HOW TO JUGGLE WITHOUT BALLS

by **Karen Haddon**

ISBN: 978-0-9931782-0-7

First published in 2015

PUBLIC SPEAKING
AND EVENTS

Karen Haddon is available for public speaking and business events throughout the UK and worldwide.

Ten percent of the proceeds
of this book will go to two charities:
Helping Paws (established in
Brighton, England) and Galgos Del Sol
GDS UK registered charity No: 1158983

For more information, please contact Karen directly at:

karen.haddon@lemaitreltd.com

This book is dedicated to the many special women in my life who have truly inspired me and to the men who have influenced my most important decisions. To my mother Olivia, who demonstrated quiet dignity her entire life and showed more strength and courage in her final days than anyone should have to. To my beautiful, precious daughter Jamie, who has given, in the true sense of the word, meaning to my life and will always be my greatest accomplishment. To my dearest sister Maxine, who's shared so many happy and sad experiences with me from childhood into adult life and who I couldn't have been closer to through my formative years, if she'd been born my twin. To my darling nieces, Charlotte and Georgia, who have both been more like daughters to me and sisters to Jamie and who've helped make my life complete. To James, my daughter's brother, although not related to me, is the son I never had and to her sister Victoria, who I've yet to meet at the time this book goes to print, but who I know I'll love and will forever be an extension of our family.

To Karen, who's been with me through thick and thin since adolescence and has just been the dearest friend anyone could wish for and to all my amazing female friends who have shared my triumphs, but more importantly, my failures. To my special boys Rick and Mick, who have both been constant male influences throughout my adult years and have experienced not just the fun, but the heartache as well. To my father, who's taught me so much, been a selfless man and a shining beacon my entire life and has remained the best example any parent could be.

Finally, to the man I share my life with, who has, without question, been my one true soul mate, lover, confidante and teacher. You alone have taught me how to openly share my innermost thoughts and feelings and above all, have shown me that real achievement only comes with great patience and personal sacrifice. I love you more deeply than any human being has the right to love another.

PREFACE

Psychology is an amazing science and I often wonder if those who've studied it and achieved degrees in the art, are actually any more qualified to understand the laws of nature, than those of us who observe them. How many times have criminals fooled the psychologists in a myriad of ways and guises? How often have we watched, for instance, a TV appeal with parents begging and pleading for the safe return of an abducted child, only to find out eventually, that it was the parent who killed and disposed of their offspring but appeared as any normal, desperate, parent would in front of the cameras? I wonder when watching those appeals, the percentage of ordinary people who actually spotted something slightly disconcerting about the parent's demeanour and how many times the psychologists missed it through over analysing their reactions? The reason for my question, is that I believe 'ordinary' people have as much ability to interpret human behaviour as many of those trained specifically to do so, but possibly on a less perceived level.

What makes someone qualified to give advice and assist others through traumatic or difficult times? Is it the 'ology' (as Maureen Lipman so succinctly described it in those old BT ads) that separates the experts from the rest of us? Are we so determined to only follow the advice of the people we believe have the expertise to interpret our minds better than we understand them, or should we simply learn to trust our own judgement and the gut instincts we were born with, but rarely heed? We're living in a culture which promotes counselling, psychiatry, psychology, psychoanalysts and every product known to man in order to dissect our thoughts and feelings, when sometimes we just need to look a little deeper inside ourselves. Perhaps, before acting on this urgent need to consult those learned enough to have acquired doctorates in their fields and the academics we believe have all the answers, we should embrace common sense, a cup of tea with a close friend and some simple practices.

I believe we all have the ability to understand our own behaviour and more importantly, the foresight to make sense of our everyday lives. We don't need great philosophers to quote profound sayings in order to mystify what's basically common sense. We simply need to observe life with an open mind and while embracing all the amazing new technological advances we see daily, we also need to welcome the changes we go through emotionally in this new age of independence and attainment. For women especially, we should find the role we're comfortable in and if it doesn't fall into a specific category, we must stop assuming it's therefore wrong or unacceptable. It's all about defining your life as you see it and not using other people's definitions to fit neatly into society, for as long as that's your goal, you'll never feel you belong, nor will you fulfil your potential. It's about accepting that in the 21st Century we have more choices than any of our ancestors could've dared dream about, but with those choices, come huge challenges and responsibilities.

This book, although not written as an autobiography, shares some of my experiences as a mother, wife and business partner, in the hope that other women who have felt as though they were drowning on a daily basis (as I often did) will take some solace in the fact that they're not alone and there is a way forward. If I can reach even one woman who may be going through similar struggles to mine and make her believe she can have a career and be a mother yet still find love without giving up her independence or compromising her goals, then my journey will seem even more worthwhile. Furthermore, if I can help one man to understand how to conquer the feeling of being emasculated simply because his wife or partner earns more and is a capable adversary, then my contribution will have been immense!

INTRODUCTION

It's hard to remember how many female friends over the years I've had similar conversations with concerning the ability to juggle a career, family and relationships while keeping sane and reasonably healthy and happy while doing so. There's no question that sacrifices have to be made to maintain harmony in all areas of your life and although there's no right or wrong way to do it, there is a way to find a balance and more importantly, to find peace of mind and happiness.

While trying to find that balance, women continue to despair at the fact they feel misunderstood by the men in their lives and so the question, which has no doubt plagued the sexes since time immemorial, continues to be asked 'Why do men and women think so differently?' Do we genuinely ALL feel 'misunderstood' by the opposite sex, or is it simply easier to blame them for all that ails us?

Even if we had the answers, we may never fully comprehend the intricacies of our incredibly different cognitive thoughts, but one irrefutable fact is that women's lives in the past sixty years have been transformed from the dutiful wives and mothers they were in the fifties, to the power hungry, high flyers of today. This has left women feeling exhilarated but tired, capable but constantly challenged, financially secure yet vulnerable, and all too often, independent but alone. Most importantly, our roles, which were once so easily defined, have lost all clarity and as such we no longer understand our femininity and even question at times whether we're the man or the woman in relationships. Millions of women out there struggle to find that stability, not only with their daily schedules, but also with their emotions and they often feel isolated as a result of taking on the world without any back up.

I've endeavoured in this book, to give my views on some of the questions my friends and I have poured over many a night with a bottle of wine (or four!) hoping we'd be visited by some kind of epiphany which would finally clarify our roles and relationships with the opposite sex, giving us the harmony we all craved. All too often, we reached the conclusion that men and women love and need each other but generally don't understand each other. For some reason on reaching my forties, I stopped wondering how to bridge the gap between the sexes, which at times appeared more like a gaping chasm and instead started looking at similarities, rather than differences, between us. I began to see with a profound clarity, things which had been an enigma to me previously. I found by pure chance the answers I'd been desperate for in my late twenties and thirties - answers which weren't the incredible revelations I'd imagined them to be. They didn't come to me in some euphoric vision, or in a moment of pure lucidity, it was more a journey that began from meeting the man who changed my very being over time and made me realize that wisdom is often nothing more than a combination of experience, an open mind, the ability to adapt and the willingness to embrace solutions, even if they're outside your comfort zone. As human beings, we often spend too much time searching for answers which are right in front of us, simply because we expect them to be more complex than they turn out to be.

Women, especially, are amazing creatures with boundless energy and sheer determination and I truly believe that every one of us has the capability to make own lives better without relying on anyone else to do it for us My wish, is to encourage those women who've yet to find that belief deep down in their souls. I've witnessed, so often, that once a woman's passion is ignited to take control of her life and make those all-important changes, the transformation from submissive to powerful is pervasive.

From the courageous women I met several times at the homeless Crisis shelter and those remarkable young people at the Prince's Trust, to my dearest friends and loved ones across the world who have helped inspire me, I hope you find true love and loyalty as I've done in my life and may you continue to grow and be role models for the next generation of amazing women who will follow.

In the words of Bella Abzug "Women have been trained to speak softly and carry a lipstick. Those days are over"

You can follow Karen on Twitter

http://www.twitter.com/KarenHaddon49

and for details of Karen's upcoming events and public

appearances LIKE her Facebook page

http://www.facebook.com/pages/How-to-Juggle-Without-Balls

CONTENTS

CHAPTER 1

IN THE BEGINNING

There was Adam and Eve, which seems a logical place to start when trying to tackle the fundamental and very obvious differences between the sexes. If it was only the variance in physicality we had to contend with, it would simplify matters but sadly, the issues are far more complex than the physical aspect alone. However, when we go back to basics and consider how nature may have been very specific in granting men and women different, but necessary life skills, in which to face their various challenges, it leaves an interesting question unanswered. Are the clearly defined male and female traits, which appear to have remained firmly entrenched in men and women throughout the ages, simply learned behaviour patterns from our forefathers, or are they genuine deviances between the male and female psyche?

One difference, which has been the cause of many controversial but comical remarks over the years, is that men have an innate sense of direction, which is something women, en masse, tend to lack. One theory is that due to Neanderthal man going off to hunt in the wild, a directional antenna was required in order to return back home whilst the woman tended her children and cooked by the fire.

One might also wonder if men's obvious reluctance to ask for directions when they do get lost (centuries later) was as acute when grunting was the main form of communication and whether they felt it was a slight on their manhood thousands of years ago (as they do today) to seek assistance when they accidentally took a wrong turn!

Identifying some of the differences between men and women, allows us to theorize about whether those instincts and abilities, which appear more honed in one sex than the other, are due simply to continual use over many years of development rather than physical, hormonal and mental differences being responsible. If it's the former, then it gives weight to the theory that "Necessity is the mother of invention" and proves that the more you need a particular life skill, the more advanced it becomes. However, there are still obvious traits peculiar to each sex, many of which have been diluted down through evolution and social changes, but nonetheless, do exist.

Interestingly, many school surveys show that boys tend to be more numerate and girls more literate. So is this general trend another example of necessity dictating the skills men and women needed in previous generations, when men worked and women brought up children? At that point, numeracy would have been imperative in the world of business and literacy would be more relevant to the communication skills required to run a household and bring up children. In one study published in Brain and Language, it states that men and women actually use different parts of their brain when carrying out the same task, so whilst it seems no studies have established a variance in the intelligence or abilities of men and women, there is a physiological difference in that men do contain more grey matter in their brains and women contain more white.

Although phraseology changes over decades, 'multi tasking' as its now called, is linked more to women than men and demonstrates that it's almost impossible to look after children without managing several tasks at once. Highlighting that through generations of requiring certain skills related to our lifestyles, those abilities can become more ingrained as a trait in a particular sex, race, or nation. The problem is that we no longer differentiate between what we see as 'natural' variations between the sexes and those which are simply learned, due to our social upbringings.

If a woman's car breaks down, she's generally no more capable of fixing it than she is of picking her nose in public (something men are highly qualified to indulge in anywhere, anytime but particularly at traffic lights!). Most women are not naturally 'in tune' with how mechanical items work and neither do they have enough interest to learn. Men however, love a mechanical challenge and will insist on dismantling every domestic appliance known to mankind when it breaks, even though they've no real knowledge or understanding of how they were built. When embarking on this great adventure, they generally lay every part out on the floor and when the item's finally put back together again several hours later, not only does it still not function, but there are now several spurious components on your carpet which no longer appear to 'fit' inside the said appliance. If your partner or husband falls into the archetypal male category, he'll of course insist these parts never fitted the appliance 'properly' to begin with and will swear blind their omission has nothing whatsoever to do with its inability to operate. This argument will be backed up by his very own brand of logic but will consist of the sentence "Anyway, I didn't break it by taking it apart, it wasn't working before I touched it".

Men of course, also feel the need to understand exactly how a car engine operates in order to drive a vehicle, whereas women see no such necessity and believe they're perfectly competent drivers without having any affinity whatsoever with the shock absorbers or head gasket. It's therefore not unusual to witness many capable, independent business women suddenly become extremely 'girly' when driving home alone and the car breaks down on a wet and windy November evening. This susceptible, seemingly defenceless creature, will no doubt be exuding sweet vulnerability and feminine helplessness and the poor unassuming man who stops to assist her, will have no clue she's in fact the same super bitch who practically removed her colleagues testicles (without the use of anaesthetic) in the board room, that very same afternoon!

The debate, I'm sure, will continue for decades to come, about whether or not we're born with different traits and natural tendencies, or whether we're indoctrinated with them through social practices. My own theory, is that it's a mixture of both. Boys hang around their fathers as kids and watch as the man of the house fixes leaks under the sink, tweaks the engine of the car and uses a spirit level to hang mirrors in the lounge. Boys don't historically get dolls as toys any more than girls get tool sets to play with, so socially, we're already gearing up the sexes to mimic the idylls we perceive is correct for their gender. I can't help wondering, if girls were to receive a toy tool set as toddlers, whether they'd be more mechanically minded and capable in the DIY department, or if it would remain unopened under the bed until replaced with something pink and fluffy. What I am sure of, is that a girl playing with a tool set wouldn't provoke the same reaction that perhaps a boy playing with a doll would and again, by insisting that dolls are purely for girls, are we categorizing and even teaching each gender to be sexist before they've even reached puberty?

Many traditional fathers would never give their son 'Baby Annabel' to play with and would no doubt be horrified if they were to see their boy enjoying the role of 'Daddy' with a plastic substitute, yet we fully expect our girls to change the doll's nappies, feed them and rock them when crying because it's an acceptable part of a girl's childhood. I certainly carried on the tradition by purchasing every doll available on the market for my daughter and as a result, by the age of four, she practically fixated on babies and at parties would be found gurgling over her friend's siblings in the pram, rather than joining in with all the other four year olds. No doubt some of her obsession with little ones was part of her psyche, which I had no influence over, but had she played with cranes and fire engines instead of dolls up to that point, I wonder if her natural maternal instinct would've been quite so alert at such an early age.

Given these obvious influences from birth, it's bordering on the ridiculous that we spend our lives declaring we can't understand the opposite sex, or the way they think and act. Is it surprising that men's caring side is so often lacking and their emotional capabilities somewhat limited? They've been brought up being told not to cry, or show emotion (perhaps less so in the last twenty years) and they've been given mainly macho toys to play with, such as plastic guns, swords and axes, which means we're all socially accepting, if not condoning, they be raised in an environment of playful violence. While girls are embarking on a caring, nurturing journey as they tend to their dolls, boys are missing out on the very building blocks associated with affection, concern and gentleness towards others.

We therefore create, to some degree, the very issues between men and women which at some point in our lives drives us all to distraction. How can we not see that the very complaints we uphold on a daily basis, about men or women 'not getting it' are often of our own making and will continue through the generations, because we believe when the sexes are born they should be treated differently?

If girls didn't sit on a Saturday afternoon with their mothers watching an old Hollywood tear jerker movie but instead joined their father and brother under the bonnet of an old MGB, would they cry so easily in later life at emotional issues or would they be programmed, like men, to shut out sentimentality and be more practical? Would they need to use their 'damsel in distress' act when the car broke down at the traffic lights on a busy Friday afternoon if they'd happily studied the mechanics of the car, as their brothers had or are females genuinely born with different abilities to males and would the majority of women never be capable to tech a car, even if they were taught?

Whatever the reasons for the divergence between the sexes, the simple fact is it exists and in order to help men and women live symbiotically and in harmony, some changes in the way we perceive each other need to take place in order to value the disparities and respect them, rather than view them as threatening and intimidating. Unless we're prepared to bring babies into the world and dispense with the differences between boys and girls as early as when we decorate the nurseries blue or pink, we have to accept that by the time they're adolescents, the differentiation is already complete.

I happen to be old fashioned in my views and believe there should and can be clear definitions between the sexes, but not because of their varying abilities. Many women I've spoken to, who were brutally honest, admitted they enjoy being feminine and relish the general effect that femininity has on the opposite sex. Some also admitted to the warm, fuzzy feeling they experience when a strong, capable man, protects them in ways their own stature usually prevents them from doing. So without changing the historic and generally acceptable way we raise both sexes, which distinguishes how boys and girls develop, the only choice, once the distinction between male and female is absolute, is to try and understand what drives each other. Maybe then we can better comprehend the needs and wants of both sexes without giving up our feminism or masculinity.

One of the most common struggles couples face today, is to find a tolerance for their partner while embracing his or her point of view, yet without it, the ability to communicate is compromised. I genuinely believe that through my own experiences and the many observations I've made watching and listening to friends, family, colleagues and sometimes, complete strangers, I now understand many of the essential, fundamental and key steps to keeping men and women together in a strong relationship, which can remain happy but above all, exciting, for many years. It isn't rocket science and it doesn't take a psychologist or a marriage guidance counsellor to fix it. It's simple, basic and includes the way we've been programmed and the many variances between men and women, whether present through indoctrination, hormones, physicality or just thought processes.

It may be true that at times we act like totally different species from separate planets, but that doesn't mean we can't live side by side in the same universe as close allies and partners. Neither does it mean that the answer to all relationship problems is the same for everyone or that there's a quick fix for all that goes wrong between the sexes. Just as planets have evolved in the solar system over millions of years, we're constantly evolving as human beings and it takes time, energy and a real desire to change the thought processes we all use in relationships, in a repetitive way, on a continual basis. Until we prevent the same situation occurring, with the same outcome, we restrict that relationship from progressing fully into something amazing. Equally, the learned behaviour we tend to espouse when we see our partners act in a certain way, has to be reviewed and amended or the final outcome, in every situation, will always be the self-fulfilling prophecy we expect it to be.

We all know the saying: 'The definition of insanity is doing the same thing over and over and expecting different results' but the fact is, we're all inclined to embark on unvaried, habitual, destructive paths and for some reason, think the outcome may miraculously change. This is another reason why cognitive behavioural therapists are so popular because many of us are aware we need to think about changing how we feel and act during crucial moments in our lives, but I don't necessarily believe we need a professional to school us. We can learn to check ourselves, once we understand it's possible to amend and re-programme our responses through discipline and the sheer willpower to do so.

When I was married to my daughter's father, there was always a pattern to the arguments my husband and I had, a pattern which became increasingly difficult to break in the sense that once a disagreement began, it went along the same route, almost as if it could find its way to the end without human intervention. As an example, my husband was always late for every appointment or dinner date we had planned, so the stage was set for the same screaming match every time we were scheduled to be anywhere. He'd arrive home from work ten minutes before we were due to arrive at a restaurant or friend's house. Knowing he needed to get showered and changed and we'd then have to drive to our destination, I'd already be angry the moment he arrived home and would greet him at the door with a look my husband described as 'a face like a slapped arse'. From then on the scene was set and there'd be no conversation between us as he drove like Jacque Villeneuve down country lanes at ninety five miles per hour, to ensure we got there before dessert was served. By the time we arrived, the tension between us was palpable and our friends would do their best to diffuse the situation, but it rarely panned out well and even though neither of us were drinkers, just a couple of glasses of wine was enough to fuel the argument which would escalate again on the journey home.

The trouble with patterns, is that although we often have a desire to change them, in a similar way to taking on New Year's resolutions, what often starts out with good intent, can be extremely difficult to sustain. It's like trying to break a long standing habit that we may actually despise, but because it's familiar to us, it's also comforting in a perverse way. Breaking habits and patterns is a scary concept to many of us because it denotes change and with it, the unknown. As time goes by and numerous arguments take place, we can also easily develop a preconceived notion about how the other person's going to react and even though we may hate knowing the conclusion to this argument will be much the same as the one before, along with that resignation, comes a degree of satisfaction that yet again, we can predict the outcome correctly. The problem with having the knowledge of how a disagreement will end generally means that even if for once your partner doesn't react the way you thought they would, you're so set on the same destructive path, that you no longer actually listen to each other anyway, as you believe you've heard the other's point of view many times before. It then becomes increasingly apparent you're more interested in getting across your specific points, than listening attentively to anything your partner has to say. Even if, at that stage, your partner's able to make a valid argument, it's lost to you as you've already made up your mind that point scoring is more important than solving the issue.

I remember on many occasions wondering how life had gotten to the stage where my husband and I simply couldn't communicate without arguing, especially as we'd both been in love to begin with and respected each other's opinions above all else. Yet within five years, we could barely speak without adding defamatory comments at the end of each sentence. My husband's pet name for me had become 'The mad psycho bitch from hell' (which was one of the more endearing terms he used!) and looking back, I believe that title had some merit. Through utter frustration, I was always simmering just below boiling point and as a result, would often overreact to a situation that today, wouldn't provoke any reaction at all.

If only I'd had the foresight to understand human relationships with the clarity I now possess, my life could've been very different. Strangely enough soon after our separation, my husband became one of my closest friends and remained so for the next sixteen years. We couldn't make our marriage work, but our love for each other was still evident in a different guise long after I left him and everyone who knows us and has met us since we divorced, has marvelled at our genuine friendship.

What many people forget when they divorce, is that once upon a time, the person you now feel the need to direct all that venom at, was the most important person in the world to you and practically your reason for living. All the qualities which drew you to each other in the first place are still likely to be there, but they've become lost to you through bitterness and in some cases, total contempt. If you peel away all the anger, frustration and hurt, which are just some of the emotions we go through at the end of a relationship, you'll see that those same qualities you once admired and fell in love with, are still present under all the acrimony. Tim was always able to make me laugh more than anyone I'd known and yet when we went through our traumatic time together, laughter was something we rarely shared in fact we barely smiled at each other. Nevertheless, once the relationship was over and we stopped arguing about the most insignificant issues, we could make each other laugh again and that's one of the most healing emotions for all concerned.

So how and when does it all start to go wrong? What are the signs that the relationship's beginning to falter and what makes the crack that begins to appear, turn into a gaping crater impossible to mend?

CHAPTER 2

SEX, COMMUNICATION AND TRUST

I believe there are three main reasons for the breakdown of a relationship and through the research I've done and the kindness of people sharing their experiences with me, I've found it's rare for these issues not to be the main culprits.

SEX
COMMUNICATION
TRUST

The majority of people reading this book will probably think the deterioration of their relationship began with lack of money because there's an argument to say that everything looks so much rosier if you can afford a nanny for the kids, have an unlimited budget for clothes and fly off on holidays whenever you start to feel the pressure of everyday problems creeping in. I fully concur that lack of money can be a factor in making life more difficult for couples, as it certainly adds to the stresses of life when you're struggling to pay for the most basic necessities, but lack of money is rarely the main cause of the breakdown and in my opinion, it's usually just a symptom.

When we start out on life's journey, few of us have money, but as young lovers, we all swear our allegiance (often against our parent's retorts that it's as easy to fall in love with a rich man as a poor one!) to stay in a cold, damp, bedsit without amenities with the man we love, rather than be out at the finest restaurant drinking champagne with a person who doesn't make our heart race. So five to ten years later, lack of money can't be blamed for the fact that not only do we no longer want to spend a night at home in what's now progressed to a warm flat, with some decent upgrades, but we'd probably sell our soul to have a night in a fancy restaurant with anyone who would take us! However strong the urge to blame lack of money, it can almost never be the root cause of what's gone wrong.

What happened to the strong belief we had when we met our soul mate that we'd give up the material things offered to us by another, in order to fulfil our heart's desires to be with the only person who made life worthwhile? Of all the women I've known in unhappy marriages, a good proportion had no money issues. The only difference in the end, was that they had to take into consideration the lifestyle they'd be giving up when the marriage ended. In my experience, the three main categories, sex, communication and trust are where the problems begin and where my advice to anyone going through marital or relationship problems, should focus their attention.

One would assume that sex is the easiest issue to deal with, after all, how complicated can it be? Well in my opinion, this is the most complex issue of all and the root cause of breakdowns in many relationships. Complex, because once it's removed, the dynamics change instantly.

If you think back to the very beginning of your relationship and how you felt when you first had sex with the partner you ended up marrying or living with, I imagine it was an exciting, thrilling experience.

You probably had an incredibly strong physical attraction to your partner and as that rapport grew, the mental connection also increased, heightening that amazing feeling which developed when you spent time exploring each other's bodies. There's nothing more electric than that initial contact you make with someone you're falling in love with. It's a great deal more than a physical act when you love a person and for the first two or three years of a relationship, sex is probably at its most exhilarating and sensual because it's still new and the love between you both is continuing to deepen. Add to that the sense of security and familiarity which makes the sex more relaxed and truthful than it was at the beginning giving you a total feeling of belonging to each other, in every sense. It's the most satisfying emotion I think you ever feel (other than holding your child when it's born which is a similar feeling of euphoria and completeness).

You therefore have a recipe at the beginning of the relationship for happiness, contentedness, security, trust and real love, which you believe if you nurture, will continue to intensify and remain unchanged as long as you have each other.

In a perfect world this would work beautifully and feelings would never get diluted due to other influences, not dissimilar to the fairy tales with the final paragraph we all loved as kids 'And they both lived happily ever after'. Sadly, in the fairy tales, they forgot to mention that the Princess in the Castle didn't have an unmanageable mortgage to pay and when the heating broke down in the castle, the man servant dealt with it not the Prince, therefore the Princess didn't spend four weeks nagging him to order the part required for the boiler or for him to arrange to get the gas utility man in, if unable to mend it himself (remember at the beginning of this book, men can fix everything mechanical and know all there is to know about heating, lighting, plumbing electrics, appliances, cars, ponds and fitting wardrobes!!!!!!!). Anyway, back to the story…….. great sex, amazing feelings towards each other, all warm and loving when suddenly reality creeps in and dinner's no longer at a nice Bistro (or even in a cold bedsit but at least at the beginning there were candles and efforts made to create your very own sanctuary) but is now a semi-warm microwave packet meal for two, often eaten in silence while watching Coronation Street.

This is of course where the opportunity comes in to blame the money situation for just about everything that ails us. We believe if we could buy anything we wanted and our partners could spoil us daily with presents and special gifts, we'd feel more loving towards them and would regain all those special feelings we had before life got in the way and even their smile began to annoy us. However, this simply isn't true and the mundane occurs just as much in rich families as it does in poorer ones. Eating out in a lovely restaurant most evenings with the same person, becomes just as monotonous as sitting beside them on the couch every night, or opposite them at the kitchen table at home. What begins to change in all relationships is exactly the same for the rich, the poor and those in between.

One of the biggest mistakes we all make when we first fall in love, is this tendency to spend every waking hour with the person who makes our heart beat that bit faster. Being away from them is hard and when the initial feelings are so 'all consuming', none of us think it makes sense to be apart for any length of time. We therefore don't allow ourselves to consider, that living with one person twenty four hours a day, whether it's our lover, twin brother or sister, mum or dad, favourite aunt or uncle, best friend or dearest grandparent, will eventually irritate us and that person will, in time, begin to invade our space. For some reason though, when we fall in love, we don't put romantic relationships in the same category as any other. We believe our need for each other's stronger than anything we've ever experienced and we begin to depend on the physical contact like some kind of life support machine, getting addicted to the constant high being with that person brings.

The strongest, most enduring relationships, tend to be those where through various circumstances, couples have been parted at times for weeks, months and in some cases, even years. I'm not suggesting this is the only way to keep a marriage fresh and new, but the principle of absence, whether by choice or imposed, is a great way to ensure you never take each other for granted. Couples where for instance, once partner works abroad for long periods, find that the precious time they share together, even years later, is very similar to the first few months of the relationship when their time together was incredibly special, the arguments were less and they appreciated and cherished every moment together. It's really important to understand the principles behind what happens when we spend too much time together and how this process changes our initial feelings from excitement, to irascibility.

I believe familiarity is what most of us crave in our lives, whatever age we are, but in some respects, it can be a double edged sword. As children, we'd ask for the same story to be read over and over again, even though we knew the ending. As adults, we have a favourite film we'll watch time and time again and still be enthralled by it, savouring all the special parts we love. It's the familiarity of the ending we all embrace and although it lacks the anticipation a new story or film brings, when we have no idea if it will be happy or sad, we still love to watch that old memorable scene. So it follows that a big part of us craves the familiar in our everyday lives, which gives us a feeling of contentedness and security. We understand that unknown quantities, whilst exciting, don't lend themselves to giving our life stability and balance. Nobody likes to live in limbo, which is why we strive to get financial surety, a home which is paid for and a relationship, which is steady. Theoretically, if we have those things in our lives, we should, in essence, be happy and satisfied. In practice however, it rarely works that way. More often than not, when we finally achieve the things we all believe we want, the familiar and comforting converts into the boring and mundane and suddenly, we feel like life's passing us by. It may be that the human race is simply perverse, hence the old saying 'the grass is always greener' but I believe it's more about taking both people and material things for granted and not counting our blessings every day.

Many of us will either have known, or heard of someone, who was not the most optimistic or positive person and yet when they faced a life threatening situation and survived it, or learned they'd beaten an illness which was originally diagnosed as terminal, found a new lease of life and embraced every day with a renewed appreciation. This is often because none of us really understand what we have until we're faced with losing it. The most obvious of all the scenarios, is that of couples who're blown apart by unfaithfulness, due usually to one partner perceiving a 'lack of excitement' in the marital home, but after having an affair and getting caught, they'd often give everything in their power to go back to how it was before they strayed, except for many it's too late by the time they realize what they've lost. So having strived to achieve the good job, a house and a loving family, how many then find that something is missing in their dream world and start looking outside the very oasis it took years of hard work to create?

This is where the familiarity and comfort we've deliberately shaped, turns into a liability, rather than an asset. The first sign is when a person starts to look at their life and wonder why everything outside their little haven appears so much more desirable, than what is inside it. It's not an overnight process and generally, before seeking out the excitement they crave, there's automatically a voice of reason affirming all that's good about what they've established, but if the discontent has started to creep in and begun to spread like a slow cancer, it takes more and more to resist the bright lights, especially when that person believes they're living in an environment which has begun to feel very dull.

It's normal for couples to experience the change from wanting their partner several times a day when first together, to no longer ripping each other's clothes off in a sexual frenzy, several years later. However, when it gets to the point where couples aren't even touching each other on a regular basis, in an affectionate way and have started to view sex quite differently, this is usually the start of the troubles. What people often fail to realize, is that even though sex may be less frequent, it most definitely doesn't have to be less exciting. Most importantly and in my opinion, the absolute key to keeping the closeness, is the intimacy, more than the sex itself. Bearing in mind that prostitutes can have sex with total strangers and have no intimacy whatsoever, we should try and remember that the act of having sex can be far less intimate than a kiss and cuddle with the person we love. So when you put intimacy and sex together, you have a strong connection, which is missing once you separate those two important factors.

The reality is that intimacy was one of the influences you started out with when you fell in love and when that's lost, a number of changes occur, resulting in a gradual disconnect between you and your partner. One of the first things which happens is the closeness disappears. You find that when you discuss things, you do so in a more distanced manner, almost as if you've disassociated yourself from the person you love and less and less do those little moments exist where you're demonstrably affectionate to your partner, even touching their arm, or resting a hand on their leg when talking. On its own, this lack of affection may not seem like a huge change, often because it's gradual and can be put down to not having enough time together, pressures of life, stressful days, tiredness etc. Furthermore, the implications of this disengagement may initially seem insignificant, but in my experience, it's the first sign the relationship's in distress and if not checked, can herald the collapse of even the most solid associations. In metaphorical terms, affection/intimacy is the glue holding you both together, so when it starts to melt away, months or even years can pass before the ramifications of its demise become clear, but once it loses its adhesive properties entirely, one or both of you will already be consciously aware the relationship's over.

Most of us have memories of when we were first with our partner and we'd lie in bed talking - maybe just before, or after sex, or perhaps when we just cuddled up and simply held each other. The point is, there'd be meaningful discussions while making physical contact. There'd be laughter and jokes about silly things, but more importantly, it would be easy to share thoughts and feelings in an intimate setting that we might not discuss over a breakfast table. What this demonstrates, is that 'pillow talk' is effectively a big part of the closeness that comes from keeping our sex life alive. People who go to bed, read then turn over and sleep, or even have separate rooms, have already disconnected in many ways without even realizing it. Those who believe sex isn't important in a relationship may be right if both parties have very low sex drives or are simply not sexual beings in the first place, in which case there's no reason why they still can't be affectionate and close as neither is sexually frustrated or resentful about the lack of sex and possibly the relationship was never a strong sexual one to begin with. On the other hand any couple which started out with sex being a powerful and important element, must find a way to sustain it in order to keep the affection and intimacy going, as this is without doubt, the lifeblood of the relationship.

SEX SCENARIOS

It's not difficult to work out that there are only so many ways to have sex, however inventive you may be, there are limitations to the number of positions you can attain and the number of ways in which you can satisfy your partner. Nevertheless, when it comes to the number of fantasies you can have, the possibilities are infinite. Your imagination and thoughts are endless and limitless and therefore so much can be experienced between two consenting adults, once you find the ability to talk openly about what goes on in your head. In my view, the greatest part of any sexual experience is the mental, rather than the physical, aspect. Someone can touch you in exactly the same way, without any chemistry or connection between you and it will never feel the same physically as the person touching you, with whom you have that bond.

Unfortunately, for many various reasons, women won't always share their sexual desires with a man. They may be scared their partner will see them in a different light and lose respect for them, or they may be frightened of rejection. A woman may also worry, if her partner's naturally jealous, that he might assume, by vocalizing her fantasies, these are acts she's performed with others and it could spark the wrong reaction. If that's the case, she should make it very clear, if she feels she can trust him to react in a positive way, that this is not something she's ever experienced but something she'd like to include in their lovemaking. It may simply be, that some women feel by openly discussing their fantasies, it makes them feel cheap and dirty and those thoughts should be confined to the privacy of their imagination, to use when they need to heighten their own experiences. Whatever the reason, women who have strong desires they'd love to share, but never do, should consider how much better their love lives could become if they openly divulged their innermost thoughts and lived out, with their partners, some of the sexual games they've played over in their head for years.

The fact is, actually living out a fantasy may never be the amazing experience we expect it to be and is often much better kept as a fantasy than a reality, but what a terrible waste to bury it deep in your subconscious, when you and your partner could derive so much fun out of sharing it.

Play-acting can bring a new dimension to your love life, its harmless fun and yet it can change that boring, monotonous, sexual pattern, into an experience you crave on a regular basis. Women are sometimes their own worst enemies, in that they complain about things being the same and they yearn to have something new and exciting in their lives, but they don't always take the initiative to make the changes. Have you ever considered turning up at your husband's place of work in the middle of the day and once in his office, opening your coat with nothing on but a Basque and stockings? The trouble is, we tend to associate doing that kind of thing with boyfriends or lovers (often when the sex is already new and exciting anyway) rather than with partners and husbands, when it's actually the latter relationship that's far more likely to need the inventive boost to kick start a dreary love life! This type of 'shock tactic' is one of the oldest tricks in the book to getting your partner interested again. It may not be innovative, but it's tried and tested and it definitely works. Imagine leaving your husband to consider that kind of image all day and I guarantee you he won't be working late that night!

When I spoke to a number of women on whether they'd ever undertake such a blatant act with their partner, the majority said they'd considered something daring but would never have the confidence to go through with it. This kind of response is one of the things that frustrates me and spurred me on to include this element in the book. If only women realized that most men would find this kind of gesture mind blowing and it would change their partner's perception of them overnight, along with propelling them to 'Sex Goddess' status. It goes without saying that women have to be smart about this kind of gesture and gauge what they believe their partner's reaction might be, along with considering their particular occupation. If your husband is a surgeon and is likely to be engaged in a long and complex surgical procedure then I wouldn't suggest standing half naked outside the operating theatre whilst trying to attract his attention through the recovery room! Neither would I suggest an MP's wife turning up at the houses of parliament, where she'll have to remove her coat and shoes to go through security and will perhaps attract a lot more attention than her husband might wish! This suggestion is to be used with each person's discretion, as I certainly wouldn't suggest you do anything which may cause traffic incidents, public embarrassments, or arrests for inappropriate attire in community areas!

We must remember through all this, that men are basically simple creatures and generally don't pretend to be anything else, its women who believe them to be more complicated souls than they really are because of our tendency to over analyse everything. Therefore, carrying out this kind of surprise will appeal to their simplistic nature, keep them interested and satisfied and furthermore, have them wondering what's up your sleeve for the next sexual encounter!

What tends to happen to all of us after a few years together is we all get complacent, bored and tired, so the motivation to spice up our love life isn't at the forefront of our minds. It's much easier to just complain that we never have time for sex and when we do, its roll on, roll off, missionary position i.e. simple basic sex, without any real connection or excitement. The type of sex, as a woman, you come to resent and only participate in to keep the relationship going and to hopefully stop your partner looking elsewhere. Hardly the best reason for having sex, so don't allow the act to become perfunctory and unappetising, which in turn will leave you feeling as though sex has turned into a necessary chore, rather than a longed for act to savour. The chances are your husband, or partner, isn't enjoying it that much either and probably longs to have his sex siren back - the one who would happily have had sex in a lift between floors and who's now likely to tell him to be quiet if he so much as suggests something risqué in a public place!

If your love life has begun to deteriorate, it's likely you're either in the category where you're having very little sex, on an erratic basis, or the obligatory kind. Either of these two categories means the intimacy has begun to disappear. It's even possible you don't kiss when you have sex and I imagine you rarely spend a great deal of time pleasuring each other on the rare occasions you participate in any bedroom action. Furthermore, I'd put money on the fact that when you and your partner do kiss, as one of you leaves for work, it's on the cheek and not the lips. When was the last time you actually kissed passionately like you used to when you said goodnight on your first few dates?

You may be relieved to know you're not alone and literally millions of people are in the same boat. As I said at the beginning of this book, it's about finding a balance between your relationship, kids, work, looking after the house, possibly caring for aged parents and many other variables that individuals have to cope with. You can and will find a balance but you need to understand that changes have to occur for you to improve your life and you also have to accept that many of those changes must involve your partner too, but this can only happen as a result of you behaving differently and adopting a new approach to each other.

The first step in changing the sexual habits you and your partner have developed, is to talk about them. No doubt you've been avoiding the subject for months, maybe even years, depending on how deep rooted the problem has become. You may even have thought of having an affair, or possibly you've already embarked on that journey, or your partner may've done so, with or without your knowledge. By the time you reach the scenario I've described where sex is extremely irregular and generally unfulfilling, it's likely that things are pretty strained between you and communication channels are weak and at best sketchy.

The strangest thing occurs when your sex life, which was once great, declines. Automatically, there's an avoidance at all costs, of discussing any subject which might instigate emotion coming to the surface. Hence my comment earlier in this chapter, that once pillow talk stops, so does the communication, at least on any meaningful level. This won't have been immediate, any more than the decline in your sex life was – it will have been a gradual separation and with it, the depth of conversations you enjoyed with your partner will also have slowly vanished.

Once you try to avoid sex because it's become something you have to do, rather than want to do, an unnatural, unspoken distance is created between you in order to ensure neither of you are put in an untenable position of having to refuse sex, better to just avoid it altogether. This means you subconsciously never put yourself in a situation where any intimacy may cause the stirrings of your partner, so in order to achieve that goal, you avoid getting too close. The end result, is you actively choose not to discuss anything which might be misconstrued as 'warm' or 'loving', just in case you give out the wrong signals. At this stage, the spiral's already begun and the intimacy and closeness is a thing of the past. Some people realize it and although they miss that part, are grateful to be out of the sex situation so may be prepared to treat it as a trade-off. Sadly, what they should be doing, is working out how to get the sex back on track, along with that closeness and intimacy they once enjoyed.

What isn't necessarily obvious to all couples is that when your sex life begins to fail, due to the communication patterns changing, one, or both of you, become more guarded and trust issues will probably begin to appear. This is the reason why sex, communication and trust, are generally the three main causes of the breakdown and are all connected and inextricably linked. They can be blamed in equal measure for changes that occur within the relationship and most couples will find it impossible to fix one issue, without confronting all three.

One of the reasons couples no longer collaborate in the same way after sex has either diminished or come to a grinding halt, is because it's rarely a joint decision for it to have become a non-existent pastime in our lives. Usually, there's some form of rejection from one party, which has happened often enough for the proactive one in the relationship to start giving up on asking or approaching their partner, for fear of further rejection. The rejected partner can begin to feel resentful, angry, hurt, mistrustful, confused and ultimately frustrated. Naturally, if any of these feelings are being experienced and they've attempted to ask their partner what's wrong and why there's no interest in any physical interaction, but have been refused any meaningful explanation, they may eventually suspect their partner's having an affair.

During the research I undertook for this chapter alone, it was interesting to see how many different responses there were from those who were having an affair. Some admitted wanting to leave and start a new life with their lover, but many simply continued on with their marriage, as if nothing at all had happened. It was even more interesting to find, that far from some marriages literally breaking down when an affair took place, many relationships flourished when this new dynamic was introduced.

I was astounded that some individuals found it wasn't difficult to carry on with extra marital activities for years and instead of upsetting the status quo, it enhanced relations and improved the situation with their partners. However, this outcome was only evident in those capable of major deception, where a person was able to ensure their partner never had a clue they were being unfaithful. I couldn't state, hand on heart, that this was a natural process for all who shared their stories, only in some cases did it seem as if the person was born to lead a double life and others clearly had to spend many months and in some cases, years, perfecting the art of lying. It certainly seemed to be true that a number of males I spoke with, admitted giving the game away almost the second they began their affair and apparently emitted such obvious signs, that they alerted their partners instantly. This group of men admitted (reluctantly) that they changed their daily patterns, their way of dressing, diet, hygiene and general appearance so significantly, they didn't require a detective to follow them and give proof to their partner, they literally shouted it, albeit non verbally, from the rooftops.

The women I spoke to told a very different story and were quite a revelation in their approach and handling of extra marital sex. Where I'd always believed men more likely and therefore, more capable of such deception, it seems the men not only found it more difficult to sustain this type of pretext and in certain cases it totally destroyed them and ultimately their marriages, but the women found it much easier to lie and did so with military precision and a ruthless dispassion. The depths to which women would go in order to deceive their partners, was considerably more extensive than the opposite sex and I found them to be far more creative, believable and subtle in their approach to these affairs. It seems there were different outcomes for many people who'd embarked on this double life. Not surprisingly perhaps, it appeared to depend on a number of variables as to whether people came through the experience of including a third person in their marriage with a positive conclusion, or not.

It seems the fundamental saviour for those who could condone their behaviour and continue on without being riddled with guilt, was simply their deceitful nature. It appears the basic requirement, for anyone maintaining a long term affair, is the ability to lie easily and without conscience. Either that, or they loved the person outside the marriage more than their spouse, but wouldn't leave their children and break up the home and just couldn't face life without the affair.

There's no question that the people fell very neatly into two different groups - those who'd maintained an affair and those who'd been unfaithful. Being unfaithful, generally meant an emotionally detached fling, which in its most simplistic form, might be categorized as a one night stand. This would characteristically (but not necessarily) take place, when one partner was away from home. A moment of weakness, a strong animal attraction, a brief encounter, a sexual chemistry hard to resist, were some of the phrases used to describe the madness which overcame those who engaged in these dangerous liaisons. The actions, however, of meeting someone on a regular basis, is neither impulsive, nor spontaneous and as such, the act of a partner having a long term affair, is perceived by the injured party, as a far more serious misdeed and therefore carries much greater consequences when uncovered. Whilst the act of unfaithfulness itself, can't be likened in any way, or categorized as remotely similar, to a person standing trial for killing someone, interestingly, the analogy of the punishment can be. When a person is killed in a moment of madness, denoted as a crime of passion, it will probably result in a charge of manslaughter being applied, whereas a pre-meditated act, which required careful preparation and deliberate actions in order to take the life of another, the charge would be increased to murder. If guilty, the former charge would carry a sentence of a few years, where the latter would generally mean life behind bars. Likewise, the punishment for a dalliance, might be transgressed to the other partner eventually forgiving, if not forgetting, a momentary lapse in loyalty and monogamy but a long term affair, with its extreme deception, is much harder for any partner to forgive and ultimately, accept. This is where the trust element can change the relationship forever.

In fact, many of those I spoke to, who eventually found out their partner had been lying for years, were almost more distraught about the deception than the affair itself. Somehow the planning, cheating, manipulation and general calculated dishonesty was more destructive to the relationship, than the sex outside the partnership.

Nonetheless, I did find that those who managed to eventually forgive and stay with their partner, reached a new understanding and strangely, the partner who'd been wronged, was often more in control of the relationship long term, than they were before the affair took place. It seems that the one who'd strayed, accepted their fate and understood that if they were to be given another chance, they'd need to earn back trust, respect and ultimately the love of their partner, all over again.

This can be a challenge for even the strongest of couples and those who succeed in getting their relationship back on track, after such a destructive force has entered their world, do so with pure determination and by digging deep to find strength in the most difficult of circumstances. The reward, nevertheless, for getting through this darkest time, is invariably the strongest, most enduring relationship any couple can have.

The hardest part of offering second chances to unfaithful partners, is learning to trust them again, as the temptation is to keep them on the shortest leash possible. Furthermore, one of the hardest aspects of the journey is finding the discipline not to bring up the misdemeanour every time an argument occurs. Before any couple decides to give a relationship a second go, after an affair's been uncovered by their partner, should be sincere about whether the wronged party, can, in all truth, start over, without harbouring resentment and anger.

Part of the deliberation must be whether theirs will be a genuine attempt to offer a real second chance, rather than an opportunity to punish their partner at every possible opening for his/her sins. Although the wronged partner has every right to be mistrustful, if they're unable to offer a free reign in the relationship, without instigating curfews and restrictions from day one, then they're not really starting over again, they're just offering a lifeline with multiple conditions.

Putting your partner on 'Parole' until such time as they've proven their worth again, is likely to work for only a short period of time, as there may be gratitude, initially, for the second chance they've been given, but they'll soon come to resent the constant reminders of their life of crime once they've attempted to 'go straight'. The problem is, the injured party will often feel their partner hasn't served their time yet and will want them to be punished for all the pain and hurt they've caused. I'd caution anyone in this position, to remember, that if you insist on making your partner serve their sentence in full, you have to be prepared for the relationship to suffer during their time of 'figurative incarceration'. Be aware that at some point, your partner may decide he or she can't live with your bitterness and the unrealistic conditions imposed and may simply cut their ties and move on.

This kind of scenario gives a demonstrable case of why sex, communication and trust are bound in a relationship and why they need to be repaired slowly, if one, or all, have been breached. Most couples, particularly men, will do whatever they can to avoid the deep, meaningful discussions, because it could result in them delving into parts of their psyche they never want to confront. Women tend to realize very early on in relationships, that men are much more comfortable when they don't have to discuss issues on an emotional level. This isn't always because they're scared, it's often because they simply don't know how to begin - it's not a natural process, so if they've never been challenged to talk about things of this nature, it will initially be a tough ask. You'll meet resistance and in some cases, outright refusal, but this is when you need to continue on your path and make your partner understand this is the only way to make the relationship work. It won't be easy, especially if your partner believes things are okay the way they are and doesn't want to engage in conversations which may uncover issues he's happy to leave buried.

Remember, the main reason couples go to counselling or marriage guidance, is to talk. It's much more about the couples communicating, than it is about the counsellor imparting pearls of wisdom which miraculously save the marriage. Simply by sitting in a room, with no distractions and having to confront uncomfortable issues, couples begin to communicate again and start to rebuild the relationship. The great panacea, for those wanting to improve any area of their life together, is to begin by talking. This simple technique, is the only methodology to repairing whatever is broken and will lead, eventually, to a better understanding of the sexes and each other. No counsellor can 'fix' a relationship, they can only give you the building blocks you need to start resolving the problems. Their role is to start couples interacting again, slowly, in order to deal with problems, conflicts and the drifting apart of souls, who desperately want to be connected again but don't know how. You don't need another person to step in and discuss the intimacy of your relationship - the two of you can do it, alone and in the privacy of your own home. You just need to reinforce the foundations you laid when you first started out on your journey together and gradually, the structure will become strong again and you'll feel so proud that you built it without any outside influences, just determination and a desire to get back what you once had.

Interestingly, since the advent of e-mails and texts, it's sometimes easier to send a message which could help you to say something you've been struggling to articulate, to your partner, face to face. Although I personally don't advocate trying to deal with major issues by text, or e-mail, I think it has its place in allowing some couples to open up channels of communication. By this, I don't mean having the entire discussion of why your marriage is in trouble via phone and computer, I mean sending messages, which may promote good relations, such as 'I love you so much and I'm sorry I haven't been able to show it lately. I'd love the chance for us to have dinner this weekend and to really sit and talk about things. There's so much going on in our lives and we don't make time for 'us' anymore. Could we make some time?' This is neither provocative, nor is it pleading. Sometimes it becomes hard to tell the person who you've begun to resent, for whatever reason, that you love them and yet you do and you long to say it, if you could only rid yourself of the anger and frustration you may feel about various issues.

Feeling aggrieved and hoping your partner will approach you so you can explain why you feel the way you do, begins to wane after several months of no reaction and women tend to do that more than men, hoping for a positive result. This is another reason why telling each other how you both feel, instead of expecting the other person to automatically know and respond to your moods, is the only way to experience an assured outcome.

Remember, the very hardest part of this entire journey is taking those first steps to re-building, or changing, a relationship. Saying out loud all those things you've kept bottled up inside, is, without doubt, the most difficult and challenging thing to do and takes real courage. I've always believed you get out of life what you put in. It's so easy to settle for things simply because you believe that's your lot in life. It's even easier to believe that if you disturb what's been resting for so long, you could find you and your partner are wrong for each other and maybe you won't be able to fix the problem, so why bring it to the surface in the first place? You may even think your partner no longer wants you but is staying with you for the sake of your children and you're scared of being alone, so would rather stay in a bad relationship, than not be in one at all.

There could be various obstacles which are stopping you from wanting to upset the status quo and I imagine they'll all be valid, logical, excuses. You might even call them reasons but they're not. There's no reason not to be open and honest about your happiness. We're here on this earth just once and during that time, we can take control of so many areas of our lives and improve them, but often we choose not to because we're either scared, or have been brainwashed to believe that whatever happens to us is destiny. I believe strongly in us taking certain pathways because we're meant to go a particular route, but in order to reach our ultimate destiny, we control so much of what we do with our opportunities, our fortunes, our lives and relationships, along the way. Meeting the person you fall in love with, is destiny or fate but keeping that person in your life and fulfilling your dreams together, is pure intention.

Everyone has good and bad times, cycles where everything seems to be against them and they feel like they've lost direction and can't make anything function or work the way they want it to. To elicit optimistic thoughts during those cycles, feels almost impossible. Even if you try and think cohesively, it doesn't always work and you can begin to believe you're cursed and have no power over whatever outside influence is interfering in your life. I've experienced those times myself and understand how very hard it is to find the positive in anything when your life's crumbling around you. Once depression descends upon you, stress creeps into every pore and life feels like you're trying to climb Mount Everest daily, without any limbs to assist, you begin to believe there's no way of improving your life and are doomed to live with misery and mayhem forever.

When I left my first husband, my daughter was only twenty two months old and it was one of the most difficult times of my life. I was working full time as financial director of our company and my daughter simply wasn't sleeping for more than two or three hours a night. I was barely functioning, what with her erratic sleep patterns and the company (which thankfully, is now incredibly strong) about to go into a voluntary arrangement. The stress of a family business, which we were trying to save from administration, organizing a house move, divorcing and having a small child to bring up alone was hard enough, but then I contracted Salmonella poisoning, was in bed for almost three months and my weight plummeted to under ninety pounds.

I'm generally a positive person but it was incredibly difficult to find any positivity in my life at that point and the challenge was to believe things would get better, when I barely had the strength to face the day ahead, never mind an entire future of what seemed, at that time, like purgatory. I remember feeling like I was failing in every area of my life, after all, I'd left my husband, was a single parent, our family's livelihood was being threatened, my health was at rock bottom and I was struggling to get on with my family, as the pressure of the business was causing regular arguments whilst we contended with trying to survive a recession and keep our company afloat. Looking back at those times, I now realize they were some of the most challenging years of my life, but by far the most character building. Most people can cope with one area of their life going awry at a time, tough as that is, they usually find respite somewhere else, but I literally found no such relief. I left my husband the day I came out of surgery to have my appendix removed and within weeks, we'd put our group of companies into a voluntary arrangement. The Gulf War had erupted and numerous bands cancelled the UK and European legs of their tour, which was and still is, a large part of our business due to us manufacturing and supplying pyrotechnics and special effects to the theatrical and entertainment market.

My daughter, coincidentally, had one of her vaccinations the week I broke up with my husband and didn't sleep an entire night again until she went to full time school, two years later. For most people, sleep deprivation is a terrible affliction and renders the majority of us incapable after several continuous days of it. To therefore be part of a decision making process in a company, working long hours and managing large parts of the puzzle, is difficult enough on its own, but without the fundamental ability to rest and restore your mind and body, it's a tough ask. I know many women have gone through similar experiences and I can only tell those of you who are going through a challenging time now, the strategy for getting through those impossible moments, is to embrace the chaos and not fight it. In order to move forward to a more structured, peaceful and contented time and not slump into a glorious depression, takes enormous effort but more importantly, great faith. The faith comes from knowing that like everything else you've experienced in life, either good or bad, it's a transient journey. Nothing lasts in its present state, it is constantly altering.

I equate the most difficult times in my life to the hardest workout I can put my body through. I hate doing it and I long for it to be over, but I know it will be and when it is, I'll be in better shape for it and will derive a certain satisfaction knowing that I made myself go through the process. I also take pleasure in recognizing I'll have done my body and soul good for digging deep and pushing myself to certain limits and I use the same philosophy for my life.

When times are incredibly difficult, I visualize how amazingly strong I'm becoming with each day that I emerge through the despair. I imagine how I'm going to feel in much happier times and how humbling it will be to have endured the tough, and sometimes very isolating, experiences I've gone through. I truly believe it's impossible to savour and relish the good times if you can't appreciate the bad. Nobody wants hardship, we all strive for good, happy lives but none of us are immune to harsh periods, whether it's due to financial issues, grieving for a loved one, illness, divorce, injustices in a family or job, or a hundred other woes that affect us all. Life is full of joy but equally full of sadness. It's how we manage the sad and difficult times that not only defines us, but dictates how much we'll appreciate the happy times ahead and it's often what differentiates the weak from the strong.

I firmly believe, that we make selective choices regarding our fragility or toughness, it's not something which is a genetic factor. Characteristics, such as being outwardly gregarious and appearing self-assured may be in our genes, as part of our disposition but actual strength or weakness shouldn't be gauged by our personalities alone, which is often the very deceptive measuring tool influencing our perceptions. Being confident and self-possessed are pure character traits, but should never be used to determine resilience, even though we tend to perceive individuals portraying those qualities to be strong. We often don't even question our strength until we need to call upon it, so we may go through many years of our lives oblivious to our true potency, convincing ourselves we don't possess it. I've been guilty of labelling a person weak and yet years later, in times of true adversity and extreme difficulty, they've in fact shown enormous strength and courage, far greater than anyone would've imagined. This is why it's so very important to put yourself through uncomfortable situations, difficult times and always challenge yourself, rather than take the easy way out.

I'm certain that many people have no boundaries, but they believe they do, which immediately limits them. One of the greatest tools at our disposal is our minds. The very reason films are so powerful is that visualisation in story telling has such enormous impact when you see an image on screen. Our minds can have the same impact, especially if we use them to our advantage by envisioning ourselves in difficult positions. Most people don't want to do it because it's deeply disconcerting, painful and can trigger feelings of despair. The flip side however, is that it can be an incredibly powerful exercise, to strengthen our resolve and put the fight back in our bellies.

It may be difficult to understand why, but when my daughter was young and I lived alone with her, I'd make myself consider the possibility of someone breaking in and threatening my child. Although some may not fully comprehend the reasoning behind this exercise, I'd very occasionally try and focus my mind on the worst scenario imaginable for me at that time, which was being put in the position where I'd need to protect my baby. It's probably the single most frightening emotion for any parent, especially a woman who feels vulnerable.

Conversely, by forcing myself to go through the awful thoughts and feelings of somebody entering our home and terrorizing us, I found I'd design various ways of dealing with it and would put specific plans in place to ensure I was prepared, should I ever be confronted with a burglar. That doesn't mean I turned myself into a vigilante and was planning on being a one woman army should a break-in occur, neither did it mean I went through each room setting 'Home Alone' style traps for an intruder! It simply meant I faced my worst fears in my head and knew that by doing so, I'd prepared myself, in some way, for the pure horror I'd feel if that situation ever came to pass. So instead of it paralysing me and overwhelming my thought processes, it equipped me to deal with the impact, if it ever arose. It gave me internal power to know, that in order to protect my child, there were no boundaries and that simple exercise alone actually taught me to understand that there doesn't have to be boundaries in any other area of life either. When you recognize you would, without question, do whatever it takes, with all your strength and might, to keep children safe, you realize you can apply those very feelings and scenarios to so many other sections of your life in terms of the determination and spirit you can use to overcome things.

Women do have particular strength in endurance, they just tend to feel that because a man is so much physically stronger, they're the ones with all the force and might. In my experience, it's the opposite. Women will cry or scream, which is often misconstrued as showing weakness, when it's simply a sign of venting. When men get stressed, or are struggling with emotions of various sorts, they tend to get into bar fights, drink heavily, or become very distant and go into a shell. Latterly, men have been more prone to showing tears, but still a woman's often blamed for being highly strung or too emotional when she has outbursts. My advice to you is never stop crying. It's the single most important way of dealing with a crisis and has gotten me through the most difficult times of my life. It has never, in my opinion, been a sign of weakness as I truly believe I'm one of the toughest people I know, but allowing your body some form of relief is essential. You can't keep a lid on a pressure cooker without a valve to discharge the steam and the same is true of our bodies, you need to allow yourself whatever release is necessary.

I would though, respectfully suggest, that you avoid drink, drugs, anti-depressants or any artificial 'alleviators' as all you're ever doing, when bombarding your body with these, is masking the symptoms rather than dealing with the underlying problem. Papering over the cracks is a short term solution, but those cracks will eventually reappear deeper and wider over time.

Remember, whatever problems have gotten you to feel the level of stress you're now facing, will still be there unless you deal with each issue individually and solve it from a grass roots basis. All you're essentially doing, when putting synthetic 'feel good' properties in your body, is making the problem seem less important. There's an argument to say that when you have too many problems to deal with, the slightest additional stress can tip you over the edge and make you feel like you're losing the ability to cope at all, but there's also an argument to say, that by absorbing something into your system, which changes the chemical balance in your brain, you're simply covering up the problems rather than dealing with them head on. Every person is different and some may require help to get through the really tough times but I'd caution anyone when taking medication for stress or depression, to try and get whatever help is necessary, by talking through the issues first, whether with a friend or a professional, to see if that assuages some of the symptoms.

If you do end up taking medication to assist you through the worst of the problems, you may feel more able to cope, but don't ignore whatever got you to that state in the first place – continue to work to fix the underlying cause.

If anti-depressants are used correctly and are prescribed on a very short term basis, then they do have their place and can be a viable tool, but they're most definitely not a substitute for dealing with issues. Never, ever, ignore problems as they don't go away, they just get bigger.

So if I could impart any advice to those of you going through any of the issues I've covered in this chapter, the most important thing is to talk whenever you can; it's not only cathartic, but once vocalized, it begins to make sense of so many things which sometimes lack the same clarity in your head. Remember, if you're in a relationship and it's going through a rough patch, for whatever reason, it will only improve by talking through whatever is causing the resentment, anger or frustration. Not every marriage will be saved, sometimes the breakdown is irreparable, but by bringing the issues to the surface, you'll either begin to work on those problematical areas and start to solve them, or you'll find out that whatever you do, the marriage, or relationship is terminal and it's time to move on to a different chapter. That revelation alone may be painful, but it also means you can hope for a much better future and once again, will be able to consider your expectations and dreams in a new phase of your life. Don't waste years of your existence, which can never be recovered, in a loveless marriage or dead relationship simply because it's more comforting than the unknown.

CHAPTER 3

DON'T BE A VICTIM

If there's one word I hate in the English Dictionary its 'Victim'; it's so against everything I stand for and everything I strive not to be. That said, we've probably all allowed ourselves to be victims in one way or another during our lifetime. Of course there are people who've had no option and due to crime or abuse, it's been unavoidable. I'm referring though, to those of us who in some way, choose to be a victim by allowing situations to arise and continue when we could do something about them. Whether this is in our jobs, marriages or another area of our lives, we have, for many varied reasons, chosen not to rectify a state of affairs because we don't want the confrontation or conflict associated with changing the status quo. I'm not referring to anyone who's a genuine victim, in the sense that they're scared and have no way out of a situation where violence is being threatened.

When I was sixteen years old, I was raped at knifepoint after being locked in a basement flat in London for many hours by a man suffering from Bi-Polar disorder, which in those days was called schizophrenia. I didn't expect to survive the ordeal, after being threatened with a slow and painful death during my incarceration. Not surprisingly, it had a seriously profound effect on my life going forward and after suffering some appalling panic attacks (not that I recognized them as that at the time) and feeling deeply distressed for many months, I eventually decided I had to do something to change my mind set about the experience, otherwise I was never going to be the person I was before the event and I certainly didn't like the person I was after it. I knew it wasn't possible to erase it from my life so I began to understand I had to find something positive in the encounter if I was ever going to recover from feeling debased and fearful for the rest of my life.

In the nineteen seventies, counselling wasn't as easily accessible as it is now and as my father was unaware of what'd happened, because my mother was concerned that as a protective father he'd take matters into his own hands and not allow it to go through the judicial system, I hardly ever spoke of it. My mother, sister and best friend were the only people who knew what I'd been through, along with a private doctor, who my mother sent me to see in order to ensure I hadn't contracted any disease. I was reticent to allow my mother to see just how deeply affected I was by the event, as I knew she felt incredibly guilty that she'd persuaded me not to make a statement to the police in order to have the man arrested. I therefore not only carried the burden of the attack, along with the inability to speak of it, but I also had to deal with the injustice of not being able to do anything about it on a practical level. Add to that, the worry and guilt that stayed with me of not pressing charges, knowing that he'd very likely rape someone else and maybe even kill a victim in the future, it was an extremely difficult time in my life that quite literally changed the landscape of my teenage years.

Looking back, this was a typical example of trying to do the right thing for family and those you love and not taking into consideration what's right for you. I'll always regret, to some degree, doing what my mother asked but that's because I've no way of knowing what the outcome would've been had I gone through the normal channels a rape victim would take. My mother may've been totally correct and had my father taken matters into his own hands (which he very probably would've done) and gone to jail for many years as a result of his actions, I would've carried that despair and guilt instead. She was also deeply concerned about my possible treatment by police and the courts, which she felt could exacerbate my already hideous experience, as rape victims were certainly treated very differently in the seventies compared to how cases are tackled today. Furthermore, as a sixteen year old who could visually pass for twenty five, she believed, in her wisdom, that I'd have been treated as a mature woman rather than a girl, so was convinced the defence would try and break me in the witness box and she knew she couldn't bear to watch that happen. I feel very strongly for all those who don't have the opportunity to do something about a terrible occurrence in their lives, especially one related to violence and/or rape, as it is difficult not to carry a sense of injustice with you forever. That may be why being 'fair' in all I do, whether it's as a mother, partner or employer, is such a driving force for me and why I'd always strive to help those who have suffered injustices through their lives, for various reasons.

So as a result of trying to deal with the permanent heavy blackness which enveloped me on a daily basis and threatened to consume my very essence, destroying any hope of normality in my life, I recognized, more by intuition than any real wisdom, a need to go through the painful process of re-living what happened many times over in my head. I somehow knew that in order to comprehend what'd caused me the most distress, I'd need to dissect the entire event, however painful, to allow the healing process to begin. Instinct told me that it was important to consider whether it was my extreme vulnerability, the fear of dying, the anxiety of the pain and torture he promised to inflict, the mind games he played with me for hours, the rape itself, or the inability to do anything about it, during and after the attack, that was the overwhelming factor in all that had happened.

After a great deal of soul searching, I finally began to understand, that it'd been my weakness in not fighting back that night, which had been the hardest part for me to deal with. There was a point during my several hours of captivity, when my captor had accidentally dropped the knife he threatened me with and goaded me to pick it up and use it. At that stage, it was nearer to me than him, as I was on the floor, having been dragged by my hair across the room, with the knife at my throat and it fell close to my left hand. In that instant, I knew that if I took possession of the knife I'd have no choice but to use it and either maim or kill him, otherwise, I truly believed he'd most definitely have used it on me. The fact that I didn't have the courage, at that time, to grab the knife and use it, was the part of the entire night which had the biggest impact on me and which I finally realized, after much introspection, was the hardest element for me to ever accept.

I only understood that to be the case, when I eventually analysed why, when looking back on that night, I'd always get to the segment in my head where he dropped the knife and then I'd change the ending by visualizing a different outcome. It was like trying to go back to sleep after a bad dream and willing another ending at the part where it all started to go wrong. I had no idea why I'd always get to that juncture and fantasize that I used the knife to command my freedom and escape unscathed. When I finally understood what everything had meant, I made a conscious decision to never allow weakness, of any sort, to be part of my character again. I may only have been sixteen when the attack happened and an inexperienced and frightened teenager, but I can never justify, or tolerate again, the weakness I showed that day.

As a result of letting myself down, I've confronted many fears over the years and pushed myself harder than I would've done had I never experienced the disappointment in my own ability to take control that night.

I thought long and hard about leaving that particular episode out of this book as it happened so many years ago and certainly isn't relevant to my life today and I also had to consider that many people who know me now, have no idea it ever happened, including my father who's still alive, so why bring up a traumatic time in my life that's long passed and no longer affects me? The reason I felt it was important to include it, was because I'm trying to write a truthful account of my struggles and how I've managed my life and found strength in the most difficult of times. That night was a defining moment for me and changed who I was and who I became as a person and by leaving it out I'd be omitting a large piece of the puzzle. Furthermore, I wanted to demonstrate to anyone who may've gone through something similar, that there's not only hope of recovering from such an ordeal but it's possible in time to move on, prosper and grow from that type of experience,

What I do know to be true is that once you've been a victim of violence, it's entirely natural to lose confidence in yourself and your ability to read other people accurately. One of the dangerous situations many find themselves in, is that it's easy, without even realising it, to give off negative energy after being abused and young people especially, can, through absolutely no fault of their own, end up attracting those who will happily abuse them again. This is often why our thought processes become so vital in getting us out of situations that can otherwise drag us down further and weaken our spirit. Sadly, exuding a sense of desperateness, which is something we're capable of projecting when we've been through a situation like that, may be picked up by others who are looking for anyone with weakened defences. That's why we hear about unfortunate young girls and boys who go from the clutches of one abuser, straight to another. Predators hunting for victims, can smell vulnerability a mile away and will seek out those doubting themselves who may be looking for affirmation of any kind.

I was fortunate in many ways, as I came from a home where I was loved and looked after and even though I didn't receive counselling for my ordeal and didn't really speak of it much, I had the time and ability to recover without pressures from outside influences. Those not as fortunate, who come from less privileged backgrounds, with no family or network structure to help them, may find themselves in a situation where abusers will pursue them, knowing they have little support and no real option to extract themselves from their circumstances. Once the abused have it firmly ingrained in their minds that it's somehow their fault (as many sadly do) it can be an uphill struggle to remove that negativity and lack of self-confidence, which would enable them to rebuild themselves and their lives. That's why I believe charities and support groups for abused or rape victims are such a lifeline and so essential to many who don't have families to lean on in times of terrible hardship.

Whilst the ordeal I went through affected me for many years and in essence will stay with me for the rest of my days, as all deeply painful experiences do, I realized in my early twenties that I wasn't really living life the way I'd done before the incident and as long as I continued to allow it to be a part of my future, I never would. It eventually dawned on me, that the man who'd in many ways ruined my teenage life and taken away my freedom of choice to say 'No' to something I didn't want to do, couldn't really have power over me in any way if I chose to disregard him, rather than fixate on what he'd done that ill-fated night. I began to see, that while I'd been physically weak in a situation, I'd been mentally strong enough to get through the ordeal and if I remained intimidated and unable to live life to the full because of my fears, then I'd accepted my role as 'victim', while he walked free and took full charge of his life.

Rape is much more about power and control than anything else and by allowing the person who perpetrates the act to flourish, while the victim slowly sinks into a quagmire of despair, is ultimately conceding to the balance of power staying with the abuser long after the attack is over. By emerging from this type of event as a stronger, more resilient person, you're empowering yourself, even if you never have the opportunity to see justice done, and by doing so, you reduce enormously, the impact of that which has been inflicted upon you.

While it's also very difficult for those who've been raped, not to associate penetration of any kind as a 'violation' after experiencing such an ordeal, eventually, it's possible to have an amazing sex life without any fear whatsoever and to learn to share your body without feeling it's being taken from you against your will. The most important message I can send to anyone who's experienced this cowardly exploitation of another human being, is to believe, as I do, that you may be unfortunate enough in life to be in a situation where you can't physically stop someone defiling your body, but you can always stop them from contaminating your mind. You and you alone, control the most important part of your being and as long as you remember that, you can overcome the physical aspect of being a victim.

Your mind is your strongest, most powerful asset bar none and it allows you to be anything and anywhere you want to be. If you have the terrible misfortune to experience the kind of violent deed that you can't prevent physically, then use your mind to transport yourself to a place where the perpetrator can't touch you. Nobody has access to what's inside your head and nobody can ever infiltrate that most sacred of places, unless you allow them to. This is again why I state that intimacy is not a physical connection, but a mental one.

There's no intimacy in any act if you don't allow it. Being raped is a sexual function in its purest form, it's absolutely never, ever, a connection between human beings and is only a momentary place you're in for the shortest time and once it's over, you must remove yourself from what transpired, almost as if you sensed the act rather than felt it. It does take time and patience to achieve that mind set and even if you're making love with someone you care deeply about who's a wonderful patient lover, it's easy in the early days after such an attack, to revert back to the panic and sexual anxiety, which can so easily be triggered without any warning or understanding and overwhelm you. In time however, with practice, some mental agility and a will to overcome the experience, it will disappear entirely and you'll feel the shroud of self-doubt lift, along with the liberation of being able to give your body willingly and in the most natural of ways, without that attack any longer being part of you or your future.

On the other hand, if you choose to remain scared, degraded and damaged after facing such a traumatic and life changing incident, then you'll continue on as a victim. If you decide, as I did, to take control again and refuse to feel like an object of prey, moving hesitantly through an insecure existence, then you'll progress forward and take something positive from an experience which could've destroyed you, but instead strengthened your resolve and determination to live life your way.

Although being physically overpowered is perhaps the most obvious form of being a victim and the one we naturally think of when the word's mentioned, there are many ways in which people allow themselves to suffer, even though they're not being mistreated from a physical perspective. I've witnessed countless women being bullied emotionally and in turn, they've allowed their partners to overpower them mentally by wearing them down until they have no belief in themselves or their abilities. This is still a terrible form of intimidation and renders people as helpless in many ways, as if they were being overpowered physically. Again, while I believe that men aren't naturally as manipulative as women by nature, I've witnessed several unions, whereby the man's married someone more attractive than himself, or considerably younger (or both) and in a bid to stop the woman from wandering, has openly begun to criticize his partner's clothes, looks, weight, hair, intelligence and abilities.

This usually starts slowly with the odd throwaway remark possibly referring to his partner's weight gain or something else which gets to the heart of the woman's insecurities. It will be said in a kindly way to begin with, usually followed with 'but I love you a bit chubbier'. In time, the seeds are planted to ensure that the woman, who's in fact far more likely to be in a position to attract an outside admirer, is the one who feels vulnerable, unattractive and eternally grateful to have someone who loves her. This type of oppression nearly always has the same pattern. It starts with the pure intention to disable a person's ability to look outside the relationship for approval of any kind. By the time the 'enforcer' as I call them, has entirely stripped his/her partner of any dignity, self-esteem, trust and finally confidence, the 'victim' is eternally grateful for any approval the partner's willing to give as they believe, without doubt, that they've no worth to anyone other than the person who's so kindly given them a roof over their head and appears to still want them.

It's incredibly sad to see how often this kind of behaviour goes on in a relationship. What's even sadder, is that when it happens to women, often they've had several children and have literally been worn down by tiredness, motherhood and constant sacrifices to ensure their kids and husband come first, thereby spending little time on their own needs. It therefore ends up being a self-fulfilling prophecy, as the woman really does stop taking care of herself and no longer looks or feels attractive anymore. This is a prime example of being a victim and even in this age of women's rights and achievements, it's a regrettable indictment of society, that most females still need to try and control their weight, wear make-up and dress nicely to feel good inside, but a man who feels insecure about himself, will often use the demise of a woman's confidence to wield power over her and the relationship. At a time when she's feeling most vulnerable, instead of helping her to feel like the attractive woman she wants to be again and encouraging her to spend time on herself to get back some of her self-esteem, he may be reducing further, her ability to climb out of the doldrums and feel sexy and therefore empowered, once again. In many cases, this is often part of his plan to keep her under his control and away from outside influences that could threaten his jurisdiction.

I've believed my entire life, that women have more power in their little fingers than men have in their whole bodies. I'm not sexist and I adore men, but I also understand their weaknesses. I have never yet met a man who could run a business, bring up children, organize and keep a household running and maintain a social life on his own, without a full time partner. Conversely, I've met many women, like myself, who've done just that for many years and during the stresses of it all, maintained their sanity and sense of humour. I've also never met a man (this doesn't mean he's not in existence, I just haven't come across him yet!) who has left his wife and children, to be alone. Men rarely leave the marital home, unless they have a woman waiting in the wings to move in with. Women, however, can be unhappy enough to end the marriage (as I did) without anybody else being involved, simply because she wants a better life and can see that's achievable without someone providing it for her.

Relying on anyone to provide us with our happiness is setting ourselves up for a fall. In exactly the same way, obtaining our confidence from others makes us just as exposed and unless our confidence and happiness comes from within, it can be taken back as easily as it was given.

That's another reason why I think women should wear what they feel happy and confident in and not be guided by what a man chooses from their wardrobe. If you only wear what pleases your man, then you feel good simply because someone else has given you permission to look and feel that way. You should be able to wear an outfit and deem yourself amazing without anyone else telling you it suits you or it doesn't. We all want to believe we look our best, but we also know what the reality is when we face ourselves in the mirror. We don't really need confirmation, but we ask for it. The trouble is, if you consider you look good but someone else tells you often enough that you don't, you start to believe them. That's how these people obtain their power in the first place. Those trapped in partnerships where their other half is dictating what to wear, have already started to lose their power and will eventually be unable to regulate their own moods, happiness and most certainly, their self-belief. Anyone who's confident, purely because someone else has supplied them with that particular attribute, is actually likely to be quite insecure inwardly.

Compliments or insults should only ever really affect us momentarily but deep down we should trust in our own abilities, be contented with our looks and genuinely like ourselves. I've seen so many women undergo various cosmetic procedures either to keep their man (never works) or after he leaves, try to fix something about themselves that he specifically didn't like, in order to get him back or attract someone new. The most attractive qualities any man or woman can possess, is self-assurance and an unerring confidence in who they are. If those feelings aren't harboured from within, then they'll be fragile at best and will only ever be on loan until they're taken back, at which time, you will be left totally bereft and demoralized in much the same way as broken dreams and promises make you feel. You can totally take command of your own happiness by having a fulfilling life with your children, career, hobbies, friends and a relationship that enhances all you do, not one which controls and destroys you. As long as you put everything you have of yourself into a relationship and don't save anything for you outside of it, then you can't really be surprised when your life's destroyed, if and when the relationship breaks down. Put yourself in a strong position and your partner will not only love the fact that you don't rely on him to be your entire world, but he'll desire you more because of your independence and autonomy.

Whatever your social or marital status, life can be incredibly challenging and at times seem almost impossible, but never fall into the trap of being a victim simply because you think you have no choices. There are always choices, often the option to change your life is the most difficult one, but if something's worth having, then it's worth fighting for. Never, ever, give up your dream. The more you envisage it, the closer it becomes. Hold onto it at all costs and don't slump into that pit of despair that's so comforting at times, because its familiar and allows you to indulge in that 'poor me' syndrome. We've all been there. I for one know all too well those phrases 'it's not fair', 'why is this happening to me' etc. It's easy to think it's 'personal' and the Gods are against you, but we all have our share of burdens and hardships, some worse than others but nobody escapes without pain and suffering - it's simply a matter of degrees.

It's often made harder when you see friends and or family, having a much easier time with every aspect of their life and you just can't relate to anyone because you're convinced you're the only person going through your particular struggles. It was during those times, usually when despair was my closest ally, that I made the biggest changes to my life. Taking charge, however small the step may be, is a hugely empowering emotion and drives you on to much greater things than you could possibly imagine.

I remember when I was seventeen years old and playing the lead role in a TV series. I'd left stage school, where I was dancing for up to six hours a day, so having swapped all physical activity for the long days in the studio, I put on around thirty five pounds in weight. When the series came out on TV, in my head, I looked enormous. I was in effect only one hundred and thirty three pounds but that's thirty five pounds more than my true weight (and what I've weighed for over thirty years) and I looked as voluptuous as Jessica Rabbit, only my waist wasn't quite so small! My boobs were literally colossal and I remember going to sleep for two weeks, every night, seeing an image in my head of what I believed I'd looked like on TV, which ridiculously, was a hugely overweight person. Furthermore, I tortured myself with the thought that millions of people had also seen me looking that way and it used to wake me up in the middle of the night and send me into a cold sweat.

That was a prime example of my terrible insecurities at that time but it was only a year after I'd been raped and I had very little self-esteem at that point and apart from the lack of aerobic exercise my body had been used to, I was also binge eating in between my panic attacks, which I thought, misguidedly, was a way of giving me comfort. Importantly, I made a decision to lose thirty five pounds in six weeks and I've kept the weight off to this day. That said, I don't recommend anyone losing weight so quickly, it's extremely unhealthy and it's rare for anyone to keep the weight off unless it's lost at the same steady pace it's put on. Nevertheless, what it did was demonstrate my determination and ability to govern an area of my life that I felt was negative. I wanted to look slim and I wanted to do it my way, in my time lines.

By making decisions about what you want to do with your life, how you wish to appear, who you choose to be with, what kind of job you want, you're managing areas of your life that belong to you and nobody else. Decisions about your looks, your career, your lifestyle, should be yours and yours alone when you're single. If you're living with parents, or a husband or wife, then of course it's in consultation with your family, as certain decisions affect them and you should never be selfish, but you should also never compromise your values or goals to do only what other people want. As long as that's your aim, you'll build up resentment and anger and spend your life in 'chains', figuratively speaking. I don't agree with ever letting people down and we should always take into consideration people's needs and viewpoints whenever we reach decisions that will affect our loved ones, but everyone has the God given right to be happy and fulfilled and that will only happen when you make choices that favour your ultimate objectives.

We should also remember that if we choose a path of complete personal sacrifice, whereby we do something purely to please someone else, then it's very likely those choices will involve an element of bitterness, leading to resentment later in life. Regrets and recriminations are not a healthy or spiritual experience for anyone.

My greatest purpose, when making any kind of decision relating to our business (which is very different to a personal one) is to ruminate on whether it's an impartial one. If my ruling turns out to be wrong, then the mistake itself (which I'll learn from) is of much less importance to me than whether I made that decision for the right reasons and endeavoured to be fair to all those it would affect. In my view, that's the best benchmark I can set for myself.

If you genuinely strive to do the correct thing for the best reasons and for the majority rather than the few and if your choice isn't motivated by greed or total self-interest, then you know your moral compass is on track and your decision will eventually be accepted. It's about thinking things through, weighing up the pros and cons and having the courage of your convictions while remaining honest and at all costs, never compromising your integrity. You shouldn't do anything purely to please others, but neither should you do something that totally benefits you without reflecting on how it affects those around you. Selfish people, who allow egoistic motives to guide their ultimate choices above what's right for their family, friends or colleagues, rarely find the fulfilment that an altruistic person does. Yet again, balance comes into play here and fulfilling your dreams and goals, while ensuring you consider the feelings and concerns of others, is how massive decisions should be made.

In the same way that being a victim will not bring you happiness or the recognition you deserve, being a self-absorbed, shallow person, will often derive similar results. Never was there a truer saying than 'Karma is a bitch' and it has an uncanny way of catching up with us all, if we live long enough for it to reap its reward or punishment on us and I truly believe it's the best equalizer that exists outside the movies!

CHAPTER 4

CHALLENGING MEN IN THE BOARDROOM

This title of this chapter probably sums up what this book has been about for me more than anything else, as so much of where I came from over thirty years ago and where I am today, is related to what's happened inside that small room, with one man who I had a fairly benign relationship with and two men who I've loved greatly, in different ways.

It's been a long and very weary journey, at times, having been in business with three male directors with whom I shared a boardroom for more than twenty years. However, I recently became Managing Director of the company which I part own with my father and brother-in-law, after our MD left three years ago and my father, retired. My only partner now is my sister's husband and although we share the same business title, he's left the day to day running of the company to me in its entirety, which has been both a gift (that I thank him for) and a huge challenge. I became a director in my mid-twenties and although in the early days I was happy and content just being acknowledged as part of the decision making team, which would shape and grow the company, it became clear within the first five years, that many sacrifices would be required in order to make such a partnership work. I knew soon after taking my directorship, that there'd be times I'd end up compromising either my ideals or my relationship with those I loved, in order to be effective in my role. There were many instances over the years where I had reason to question my own sanity in taking the decision to be in business with those closest to me and whilst I'm a person who doesn't believe in regrets or recriminations, on those memorable days where I thought I'd practically lost my family over my stubbornness and determination to stick to my guns on certain issues, I did wonder as I lay my weary head down to sleep at night, if I should've taken a different path. Looking back now I wouldn't actually change a thing, as I've stated already that every negative can be turned into a positive, if you can see through the despair and learn to find solutions rather than problems. In order to do that though, you have to be disciplined and must establish the fortitude to keep moving forward while you're slowly sinking into the quicksand of stress and emotional annihilation.

Thirty three years ago, very few women were in a position to receive a directorship and I, like anyone else, had to struggle to obtain mine even though it was a family business and many may think it was always going to be a natural progression to receive one. I had to earn my stripes just like anyone else in a start-up company. I began practically by undertaking whatever tedious jobs required doing in the office and worked as a junior amongst six senior women, one being my father's sister. I gradually learned the bookkeeping processes and figured out how the computer functioned, which in those days was as large as a grand piano taking up the entire end of the accounts office. My Auntie Doth was adamant that she'd never succumb to the charms of this new technology and treated it with as much caution and respect as a zoo keeper might proffer to a hungry, caged lion, in his care.

My Aunt was a dying breed who didn't even trust calculators in the workplace, never mind the gargantuan sized computer which was situated close to her desk. She continued to manually add each column of figures in her head after using the calculator, just to make sure it wasn't malfunctioning and was providing the correct answer. I truly believe she'd have remained using an abacus, given the choice, mainly because she was totally mistrustful of anything mechanical which didn't rely on pure brain power to function. By not bowing to the pressure of bringing herself in line with technological developments, her mind remained as sharp as a pin and however fast I became on the calculator, which was not unimpressive when using it on a daily basis, she could almost match me by habitually adding columns of figures, at frightening speed, in her head.

Eventually, I'd learned enough about the accounts department to be offered the role of financial director and the opportunity to purchase my first shares in the company. I sold my car to raise the money and took a loan for the remainder of the debt and my father also very kindly gave me some shares to help me on my way. It was a struggle in the early days to make ends meet and I remember constantly being in debt throughout my twenties as a result of buying into the company and trying to secure my future, but it was without question, an exceptional opportunity and I knew I'd never be happy unless I could own a part of the company that I was sharing responsibility for.

It was by no means an easy ride being a female director in a very male dominated industry and I had to spend huge chunks of time fighting my corner in order to be taken seriously. Like any minority of people, be it due to race, religion, disability or gender, you're constantly striving to be heard when you rarely have a captive audience. For me, the moment I found my voice and changed the perception of those around me, was during a visit to the bank with my father. We'd been called to attend a meeting with the manager, along with the faceless decision makers who generally remain anonymous, after we'd reached the conclusion we needed to seek a voluntary arrangement when our company was struggling to meet its debts. For those who don't recognize that term, it's when a company requests permission from their creditors, to pay back all the money owed to them over a period of time, in order to allow the company to trade out of their financial difficulties.

We owed the bank approximately £700,000 at that time and the only security they retained was the land our factory in Peterborough was built on, which was already mortgaged with them. My father, my sister's husband, our accountant and I all owned a quarter of the land each, but the majority, was at that time, mortgaged with the bank. Our company accountant had discussed the matter with the bank before the meeting and had approved us to sign the documentation when we arrived.

We attended the meeting as requested, along with the accountant who was handling the VA, on our behalf. When we arrived at the meeting, I had a very uneasy feeling which I couldn't put my finger on, all I can remember clearly is that it persisted during the pleasantries. After the formal greeting, we were offered refreshments before taking our seats at a large boardroom table occupied by at least ten people. My father and I had also been summoned to a meeting two weeks previously, as being the financial director of the group, I was naturally involved in the handling of anything pecuniary. During the previous meeting, we'd been hauled over the coals like naughty school children being chastised for misbehaving and there'd been no pleasantries during that hour of pure interrogation, so I found it quite disconcerting to suddenly be treated with such careful consideration, when less than a fortnight before, utter disdain is the closest description I could use for the reception we received.

The bank confirmed that this meeting had been called to simply 'tie up some loose ends' on the mortgage, which had been in place with the bank for several years. This, they said, was backed up by the papers they began so distribute to myself, my father and the accountant to look over before requesting they be signed by two officers of the company.

My father, a very successful and capable businessman, read his copy then signed it and passed it across so I could append my signature. As the form was placed in front of me, I noticed the table had fallen silent and all eyes were focused on my movements while an air of expectation hung heavily in the room. Bearing in mind I was still fairly inexperienced in business and was in one of the most intimidating situations imaginable, I really just wanted, with all my heart, to sign the document and leave as quickly as humanly possible. My instincts, which in the moments prior to my father passing me the forms, seemed not only to be significantly heightened, but suddenly felt like they were taking on an entirely new energy, told me vehemently not to sign the paper and to refuse, however much pressure was brought to bear. I remember slowly raising my eyes to face the room and stated, with as much conviction as I could convey, that I'd prefer to take the papers away to review everything, then I'd sign them and get everything back to the bank as soon as possible.

It took literally seconds for the atmosphere in the room to change from amicable to hostile. My father, who was clearly embarrassed and confused by my refusal, told me it was fine to sign the papers and suggested I go ahead. I wouldn't be swayed and explained I'd prefer to take them away and would sign and hand deliver them, if necessary, after I'd gone over everything carefully. An onslaught of comments were then thrown at me, including accusations of delaying a simple paper exercise, which would cause them issues if no signatures were forthcoming. Furthermore, they expressed how unacceptable this stance was, given that they'd been so supportive to our business etc. etc. They continued to heap more pressure on me by communicating their belief that it was a small gesture of goodwill to sign papers that the chairman (my father) and the accountant dealing with the voluntary arrangement had checked and agreed upon. As embarrassed as I was and as difficult as it felt not to give in to the pressure of the situation, I remained stoical about my decision, proposing that we leave, with a promise to get back to them the following day.

The meeting was quickly disbanded and once again, the atmosphere reverted back to how it had been two weeks prior when there'd been no attempt at civility and I realized at that point that the pleasantries of the day had been nothing more than a façade to make us feel relaxed in order to let our guard down.

I'll never be able to give anyone a logical explanation of why I wouldn't sign the papers that day, but the end result was, that simple refusal saved our company. I knew, by intuition alone, that there was something amiss, and without any knowledge or proof, I told my father as we left the bank, that they didn't have the security in place on the piece of land which was worth all the money. He thought I'd gone mad and said that simply wasn't possible, as we'd signed the deeds to the property over to the bank several years previously when it had been mortgaged and the papers proved that to be so, but I knew in my heart that couldn't be correct. I called the bank the very next morning and asked to see a copy of the deeds to the land. They sounded extremely evasive when they replied that the information was in storage and it would delay matters even further to find archived documents. I stood firm that I couldn't sign the papers until they retrieved them.

I collected a copy of the deeds that afternoon and it transpired that there were two separate parcels of land on the several acres we'd purchased and only one had been mortgaged with the bank years earlier, which was a tiny piece of land, worth almost nothing, whereas the large chunk of land with the factory on it, had in fact, slipped through the net. Due to an administration error on their end, it had left them with no security at all on the larger portion, causing the bank to be vulnerable and therefore unable to do anything but support the voluntary arrangement. Had they obtained our signatures on the documentation that day in their office, they admitted their plan had been to take the company and the land and sell it to recoup the money we owed them at that time. The reasoning behind their deliberate deceit, was explained to me by the bank manager in the simplest of terms after I confronted her regarding their underhand dealings; 'We weren't asking you to sign anything you didn't believe was in place with the bank already!' was her terse and unapologetic reply. Hardly a transparent way for the bank to conduct itself and not exactly the honest and open face of high street banking we all signed up to when they secured our business!

However, the outcome of the entire debacle, was that by removing that option to the bank, they had no choice but to allow us the opportunity to trade out of our problems and a few years later we were in a strong and independent position where we were no longer obligated to stay with them, so we moved to a different bank and never looked back. The moral of the story is that men and women should listen to their instincts, we've been blessed with them for a good reason. If something doesn't feel right, then the chances are it isn't. Don't be talked into making decisions against what your gut tells you, particularly women, as it seems we've been provided with a genuine antenna or strong transmitter, which can't always be explained but can usually be accessed. Even if it doesn't always make sense, listen to it and check things out more thoroughly before committing to anything.

Going back to the events that happened when I was sixteen and trapped in a basement flat just off Baker Street with a successful and well known hairdresser, who turned out to be one of the sickest, craziest people on the planet, I remember telling my best friend that very morning that I really didn't want to go to London for the date I'd accepted that particular Sunday, as something just didn't feel right. I wish now I'd paid more attention to my innermost feelings as I could've saved myself from going through a life changing event, had I understood my response, was in fact, a genuine warning signal.

My colleagues certainly changed towards me from the day of the bank meeting going forward and if I didn't feel comfortable about a situation, they listened intently to my concerns. Instinct isn't something which is logical or scientific and consequently, it's extremely hard to make a strong case in its favour, especially when you can't offer hard facts about what exactly feels wrong.

It's therefore easy to dismiss emotions and try to convince yourself that whatever underlying doubts you experienced, were fleeting and without basis, but those impulses can keep you alive in extreme cases and should never be rejected.

It may be that women's instincts are more acute than men's because of the 'sixth sense' required as a mother. Often when a baby's sick, a father will put it down to teething, colic or a minor ailment, which may well be true, but how many stories have we heard where a mother, even after a hospital or doctor has thoroughly examined a baby, knows that there's something more seriously wrong with her child and has persisted, even against medical opinion, until tests proved it was an illness as dangerous as meningitis? It's an innate sense which can't be taught and can't be logically examined.

Back in 2007, we ended up in major litigation with our business partner in Canada when he decided to purchase a pyrotechnic manufacturing plant in America with half our money, to compete directly against us. He specifically went against all our contracts and ignored our fifteen year partnership, flouting every agreement we'd ever made.

When we consulted a Canadian lawyer, he advised us to meet with our partner and try to negotiate whatever kind of deal we could, as he believed the contract we had in place simply wasn't strong enough, in law, to stop him. My partners and I were incensed and knew we had right on our side, so with the board's approval, the M.D. and I flew to Canada the very next week, met with new lawyers and obtained an injunction to stop him purchasing the plant. Sixteen months later, I was still flying back and forth to Canada dealing with the litigation, which had become extremely complex and incredibly time consuming. On one occasion, my return flight was delayed thirteen hours due to bad weather and whilst sitting in Toronto airport, I heard a man on the phone next to me who was clearly a very erudite, but aggressive individual, slightly arrogant but as it turned out, with good reason. When his conversation finished, I asked if he was a lawyer, he confirmed he was and said he was flying to the UK to deal with a high profile international case. I explained I was in the middle of litigation and had just flown in for the day to attend mediation with our Canadian partner and respective legal counsel and that it had been unsuccessful and the matter was now proceeding to a full court hearing.

I remembered thinking how strange it was, that out of all the people I could've sat next to in the airport, I found myself beside a highly qualified, well respected litigation lawyer, who I knew, from the moment I heard him speak on the phone, was the person I'd choose to represent us in court.

Again, I knew it would be a difficult conversation with my partners, trying to explain why I wanted to change legal counsel sixteen months into the litigation, with all the twists and turns the matter had taken, but when I told them that my gut instinct strongly suggested we needed to do this to win the court case, they agreed, even though it was a costly exercise to get the new lawyer fully up to speed with the case.

I found it incredibly tough telling the two lawyers I'd been dealing with for nearly a year and a half, that they weren't going to have the opportunity to see the work they'd done through to its conclusion and I was only too aware how deeply disappointing that news was for them. Nevertheless having learned to trust my instincts, even on the very arduous decisions, I didn't allow myself to dwell on the emotional aspect of how I felt about the people I'd gone through the experience with. I had to exclude any sensitivity I felt towards them, and do what I believed to be correct. I totally respected and admired both the lawyers I'd worked with and had become quite close to them through all the ups and downs of the various hearings we'd been through together, so it was a tough call, but I knew I couldn't spend too much time analysing it as it's important to remember that your first instincts are usually correct.

Again, I had to do the right thing for myself, my partners, the company and all the people who worked for us and depended on their jobs. I listened to my innermost feelings, considered the information I had to hand and made the decision. I can't be one hundred percent sure if the result would've been any different had we not changed lawyers, but I'll always believe that heavy snow in Toronto that day, which triggered a flight delay and my chance meeting with David, coupled with my instincts, had a far reaching effect on all our lives for the better.

When the court case was over and the verdict came in several weeks later, the outcome at least justified the decision to change counsel mid-way through. After two of the most stressful years of my life, I was able to breathe a sigh of relief when the result was delivered and the Judge found in our favour. Although my partners were totally supportive throughout and backed my judgement even when I had no real evidence to prove it was the right way to go, which I love them for, it was still a very lonely journey at times. Carrying the kind of responsibility which could've made our company extremely vulnerable had I miscalculated any factors that may have influenced the final upshot, meant I was accountable and nobody else, even though I always sought my partner's agreement and blessing. Being constantly aware of what an enormous impact it would've had on everyone's future, had the decision gone the wrong way, was a heavier burden to carry than even I realized. It was only after the case was concluded and I finally discharged that obligation, that I noticed I slept soundly for the first time in twenty four months.

Spending so many years in business with both my father and sister's husband, I remember many times over the three decades, when I didn't always think long or hard (enough) about challenging some of the decisions that were being made in the boardroom and which I didn't necessarily agree with. Whilst I acquired a huge amount of knowledge and invaluable experience during those meetings, I know there were moments I could've let certain issues lie and 'chosen my battles' more carefully, or at least prioritized those important times when I should've fought harder, or backed off completely. I was so determined my viewpoint should be acknowledged, that I often lost sight of any meaningful strategy and just got 'stuck in' like a street brawler. As already stated, I don't have regrets, and as the closest person in the world to me has often said, if you could ever go back and consider changing, through choice, just the negative aspects of your life, that would automatically have an impact on the positive elements too and ultimately reshape the outcome of everything. I agree with him and truly believe that the good and the bad, although not always measured equally in life, fashion us irrevocably and neither should be meddled with, even if we did have the power, in retrospect, to change things.

Although, in my more wistful moments, I imagine a time when I didn't antagonize my father as I so often did in those situations, because I know that by doing so and by habitually insisting on doing things my way, to prove a woman could be as successful, if not more so than a man, I sacrificed a part of my relationship with him that I can never regain. I would've loved to show him on occasions, that I was still his baby girl who looked up to him and was always seeking his affirmation, but I couldn't find the right words or the correct way to do so, without conceding weakness. That was my failing and I see now that by being unable to communicate my true feelings, partly because I was scared they would put me at a disadvantage, I lost forever an opportunity to be the daughter I could've been, at the same time as being a worthy adversary and business partner. It wasn't as if we spent our entire lives arguing, we did of course have lots of wonderful times when business issues were left at home and we enjoyed some amazing holidays as a family, along with our Christmases, which were always extraordinarily special. It's just that it's not a natural course of events for a daughter to challenge her father in the way I did, especially an adept and accomplished businessman, with far more life experience and influence than his daughter had.

I have real empathy for anyone in a family business, as it's an impossible situation at times and although it can be incredibly worthwhile to share the successes of a company with those you love most in the world, there are tough choices to be made when you're trying to be your own person and make your mark in the business arena. It wasn't until after my father lost his ability to debate when he developed dementia, that I began to feel the real burden of guilt about the level of my tenacity on particular occasions. Hindsight is of course a wonderful tool to measure our successes and failures by but doesn't assist us in doing the right thing at the right time. Although I definitely don't miss the disagreements we had, which in my younger days had caused me so much distress and at times, real feelings of isolation, it's fair to say that in watching my father's personality change from the powerhouse he'd once been, to a nonthreatening, almost submissive person, I've genuinely ached to have back the man, who, in so many ways, shaped me and helped me become the person I am today, even if that meant I'd have to face more passionate arguments with him.

The most significant problem sitting across a boardroom table from your father, or anyone you have a relationship with outside business, brings, is that the pure familiarity of that tie, allows you to communicate with a much less guarded approach. Remarks become personal, professional lines become blurred and suddenly you're using delicate, private matters to give weight to your disputes, disregarding all acceptable boundaries, as long as you can prove your point and win. The best analogy I can think of, is that normal board directors with no personal affiliation to each other, tend to stick to the confines of a structured framework in their discussions, adhering to all the rules in the handbook. Not dissimilar to the guidelines in a world boxing organization, where contestants are bound to only throw punches during the designated rounds in a respectful and orderly fashion. However, once family board members get involved, the gloves come off and it's like entering an illegal cage fight where no regulations apply and every form of combat is acceptable. My father and I both adopted that approach in some instances and while I believe he admired and respected me for my resolute willpower and determination to conquer all, he also disliked me intensely at times, as I did him, even though our love for each other was as fierce as our arguments could be on occasions. What we did find for each other, was a mutual deference, and I was often amazed at how quickly my father would grasp a situation in the early days and find a fast solution that covered all the bases. I was in awe of how he proved, many times over, that he was a force to be reckoned with and wouldn't take any prisoners.

I learned that being highly educated, while a great asset in business and life in general, isn't always the driving force or the only key to success. My father, much like myself, left school at fifteen (although we did so for very different reasons) and he demonstrated on a regular basis, that he could outmanoeuvre some of the most qualified people, with street smarts and his ability to read situations. He showed me how to utilize whatever tools were available to me in order to be successful, to work all the hours God sent and to ensure we were surrounded by an amazing team of loyal and talented people (which Rick and I have working for us and are eternally grateful for) giving stability and continuity to our business. There's no better, sound advice to give another person than to assume those procedures and watch the world flourish around them.

Another vitally important lesson I've learned in the last ten years is not to confuse those who are naturally ambitious, with those who are extremely driven, as they are entirely different qualities, yielding distinctively diverse results. In my humble opinion, achieving affluence through any means available, is how ambitious men and women operate, whereas driven people's incentive is much more about success than money even though wealth is often a natural derivative of their toils. Athletes, sportsmen and dancers are usually highly driven individuals but their goal is rarely to acquire great riches. Being at the top of their chosen profession, winning trophy's and receiving accolades by their peers, is generally their motivation for the thousands of hours they invest in training to reach that kind of attainment. The wealth they may eventually acquire, through their dedication, is rarely a driving force in what they do.

I've always been more driven than ambitious, as my personal success and that of our company, is a far greater purpose for me than the money it may bring with it. I see ambition, all too often, as an injurious force in an individual and those displaying it, will often possess ruthless and selfish tendencies. This is mainly because, as long as money is the driving factor in decisions we all have to make, especially in business, then greed will never be far behind it. Once you introduce that most destructive of stimuli into the equation, you develop a very subjective thought process with a contaminated view, which will have lost its fairness and objectivity. I believe ambition should be one of the seven deadly sins, as it ranks just as highly as greed and gluttony to me – both being self- absorbed and unattractive qualities. Again, many ambitious people don't care how they achieve their assets, as long as they get them. That usually means that they'll play dirty, because while some may be hard workers, many aren't. I've met several who are prepared to marry in order to obtain the funds they desire or will acquire them through whatever unsavoury method becomes necessary to satisfy their requirements. Let's be honest, the history books are littered with those who have slain their adversaries for cash and the courts across the world are awash with many who have killed business partners or husbands and wives to gain it. Driven people though, are far more likely to want to achieve wealth through their own hard work, determination and skills and that's why I would never choose to have an ambitious person working for me, as those I've met through my life have proven that they'd sell their own mother into slavery, if they could get the right price. Not a quality I revere and most certainly not what I'd be looking for when employing anyone on my team.

Back in 1997, after finding a manicurist in the Yellow pages, I went to get my nails done for a ball I was attending at my daughter's school. I turned up to my appointment, blissfully unaware that it was about to herald a totally new chapter in my life. While I sat having a very unremarkable treatment, I remember thinking, as I listened to the wonderful woman who was filing and polishing my nails, that it was rare to find a person you hardly knew, but liked so much, you couldn't imagine them not becoming part of your life. The lady's name was Janet and within six weeks of me attending my first nail appointment, we'd agreed to go into business together and had already begun the process of setting up our new company.

Her husband Trevor, who much like me, was involved in a successful business, was also going to be a director of the company and they'd already considered starting this new business in the cosmetic surgery industry, before I'd even set eyes on them. After Janet and I established such a strong connection from the moment we met and I was so incredibly enthusiastic about their idea and the product they were going to market, we made an instant decision for me to be part of this new venture.

I immediately set about raising money to put into the corporation, in order to obtain forty nine percent of Rubicon Medical Ltd., which was to be a cosmetic surgery company offering a brand new, truly extraordinary face treatement, and which ended up revolutionising chemical peels and practically eradicated laser treatments for many years after it hit the market. With a great deal of hard work from both Janet and I at the inception of this new enterprise, we launched the face peel of all face peels, which literally took the cosmetic industry by storm and was featured in all the major newspapers and magazines across the UK and even in the States. The product was so unique and the results so astonishing, that the journalists covering the articles had some concerns about the authenticity of the photographs we presented to them. They decided therefore, when writing their features, to follow individual patients through the entire process, using a photographer from their syndicate, to take the 'before' and 'after' shots, in order to validate the results. Several of the journalists named the procedure the 'miracle mask' after reporting that ten days following treatment, the patient literally looked thirty years younger.

Janet and I still agree that even today, almost twenty years on from launching it, we've never seen a better outcome with any type of cosmetic procedure and considering there was no actual surgery involved and no general anaesthetic administered, it was even more unbelievable that the results were so outstanding.

After the first couple of years, Janet ran the company in its entirety and was a superb partner to have. She was scrupulously honest, hard-working and the patients loved her. We eventually had several surgeons working for us, all majoring in their unique specialities and although it took time to develop the various procedures we undertook, gradually we built up a great reputation. After carrying out hundreds of cosmetic processes, from facelifts and breast augmentations, to liposuction and even penis extensions, we developed a database of many delighted and highly satisfied customers.

Sadly, in 2011 when the PIP implant scandal erupted, our company, which had used those implants for many years, became victims in this underhand, fraudulent scam and we had no choice but to close the business. We did all we could to try and rectify the situation for the patients, who had unknowingly consented to accept industrial grade Silicon instead of pharmaceutical grade, as had Rubicon itself, believing them to be CE marked and approved medical implants. It was an impossible situation and after consulting a barrister in London, we were advised to close Rubicon down. It was a terrible time for both Janet and I, as one of the reasons we'd set up the entity, was to genuinely help women and men feel better about themselves. There's nothing more rewarding than to see a person who for instance, has had the most awful complex about their face or a part of their body for many years and has finally taken the step to rectify something which they've lived with, unhappily, since birth. The thought that we'd unwittingly done anything to our patients, many of whom had become friends, as well as clients, sickened both Janet and I and I know she found it incredibly hard to come to terms with after working so hard for many years, to build up a good, solid business.

We gained a lot of knowledge along the way and had the PIP implant scandal not ruined Rubicon's future, I believe it would still be one of the most respected, cosmetic surgery companies, in London today. One of the best things to come out of the entire experience for me, was that I found Janet, who's one of the nicest people in the world and will always be a dear friend. I also received further confirmation that my instincts had once again, served me well. I put my faith, without much evidence, into a business venture with a virtual stranger, but I knew almost instantly upon meeting Janet that I could trust her with my life and that whatever happened from that day on, she'd watch my back.   Through some really unfortunate circumstances, we lost a good business and a great opportunity for future growth, but we stood side by side from beginning to end and I learned a lot about the cosmetic surgery industry and secured a lifelong friend, which was far more enriching than anything I could've gained in monetary terms.

Since the day of the bank incident, I also learned one of the most valuable lessons of my life. Even if I feel out of my depth or don't feel like I'm grasping a situation, I pay attention to my gut. I'm not embarrassed to challenge anyone and ask questions which matter and I certainly never feel pressured to do anything I'm uncomfortable with. We all get hunches from time to time, in some people, the feeling will be heightened or more refined than for others, but If you're looking for an edge in business to give you an advantage, listen to your God given instincts and learn to trust them, they're there for a reason.

CHAPTER 5

BALANCING THE BOOKS

Everyone who understands even the most basic concept of finance, is aware that books have to balance. Double entry bookkeeping is as old as the hills and in general terms, means there must be two entries on either side to balance each transaction. This is no different in every area of life. I remember years ago, a wonderful bank manager, who became a good friend, told me after six months of opening my account that he was sending me another cheque book, which was my third in as many months. He explained that he was also enclosing a paying in book, even though he felt I must have lots of space left in the first one, as he hadn't actually seen any sign of it being used! He then very graciously reminded me that I might want to consider paying some money into the account, to compensate for all the money I was extracting from it, or more to the point from my overdraft facility, which in those days was pretty easy to obtain.

It's the same principal for everything we do, there needs to be equilibrium and when there isn't we feel out of kilter. We've all heard the cliché 'Everything in moderation' but rarely do we heed those wise words. How ghastly do we feel when we sit down to a big meal and consume far more than we really need? How ill are we the day after drinking excessively, even though it seemed like a great idea at the time? How stressed do we get when we engage in far too much work and don't include some relaxation time? The list is endless, but what I came to realize many years ago is that while we don't necessarily choose for our life to go out of balance, it does happen at times and not always because we've indulged in too much drinking or eating but more because life simply throws us a curve ball that we weren't expecting and certainly weren't ready for.

Anyone who's brought up kids, had a stressful job or managed a business, had money worries, dealt with health issues for either them or their family, been divorced, lost a loved one, moved house or faced numerous other stressful situations, is only too aware that stability can be lost easily over days, weeks or even months. I found out a long time ago, that there are ways to handle the imbalance without it creating serious illness, chaos, meltdowns, or all three!

Again, my experience of finding some inner strength and peace when the entire world feels like it's imploding on me, isn't a complicated process. The first step to reinstating the balance, is to find out where things have gone out of sync. Sometimes there are so many variables to blame that it's hard to distinguish which element has actually tipped the scales and thrown you off, but just like everything else in life, this is the time to sit down and work out, in which particular order of priority, matters need to be addressed. I know for me personally, that when I've found myself drowning with the unenviable weight of stress and have felt utterly devoid of any optimism, they're the times I've had to evaluate my life and make some harsh choices. As stated previously in this book, the most challenging times have really strengthened my resolve and been the moments I look back on as my most illustrious.

For instance, when my mother died, like all of us, I lost a part of me. My most solid influence was gone. The only person I could confide in who'd never judge me whatever I may've done. Inside I felt inconsolable, damaged, broken and absolutely desolate but after crying for several days until there were no tears left, I started to feel that taking on my mother's mantel was the most positive thing I could do. Negativity, is such a destructive emotion and has no place in healing. I couldn't bring my mother back, it was a fait accompli that she was gone forever and nothing I said or did could undo, or change that fact. I knew I'd miss her forever more and I'd want always to have her be a part of me. I wanted to remember her in detail and with good humour and grace. I needed to do right by her and keep her spirit alive and by thinking about what she'd want and how she'd expect me to be, it stopped me feeling helpless and racked with grief. Instead it gave me huge courage and strength to continue with every day matters again, which in turn allowed me to assist my father in dealing with the loss of his wife, my daughter to cope with the passing of her beloved grandmother and my sister and I to bond again as we united the entire family in our grief.

By understanding that you must focus on the things you can change and let go of the things you can't, positivity is naturally resumed. By making one small adjustment, you can make a big difference to your mind set and your stress levels. I'm not a negative person by nature but just like everyone living and breathing, when things get on top of me I can succumb to those feelings as easily as everyone else. Sometimes its hormones or physical imbalances that precipitate the deterioration in my thought processes and sometimes its circumstances which dictate the pessimism that roots itself inside my very being, but now that I'm aware of the pattern, I understand it's a phase and that adopting negative thoughts, however they manifest themselves, is partly my own doing. I can therefore quicken up the process and remove it.

Nobody expects anyone to feel happy after they lose a loved one and it certainly took me several years to honestly say I felt joyful again, but that part was pure grieving and missing my mother, which is a natural, healthy, response to losing a person that meant the world to me. It's even 'normal' to go into a depression but that's the part that doesn't help. Just because it's normal to be depressed, doesn't mean it's correct and it certainly doesn't mean it demonstrates how much you loved that person, as the last thing they'd want is for their loved ones to feel desolate and stop living. I appreciate that losing a parent is expected by all of us, especially when we reach a certain age, so I understand that losing a child, sibling, husband or wife, is very different and I wouldn't attempt to suggest that my loss could be compared in the same way.

I do however, have the greatest respect for those who have lost their offspring and immediately embark on a campaign of some sort in their child's name, to ensure that their passing wasn't in vein. That's a truly amazing way to find something positive out of the worst possible event that can happen to a human being. The point to all of this is that we have the power to make the best, or the worst, out of things that transpire. We can't change events, but we can change how we deal with them after the fact.

Being depressed, is often another way of saying we've lost our purpose in life. We all need a reason to get up in the morning and sometimes when that reason's taken away, we lose ourselves in self-pity and our direction changes almost immediately. It doesn't matter what our purpose is, one person's isn't greater than another's, but it's a vital element in all our lives, whether it's to feed our kids, get up to walk the dog, be a lollypop lady helping youngsters across the road, or closing a multi-million pound deal. The fact is that someone, somewhere, is depending on us to make a contribution, which in turn gives us a role in life, affirming our need to be alive and making us feel like what we do really counts.

When we convince ourselves that nobody would even miss us, let alone believe that anyone would rely on us for anything, it's easy to lose our resolve and give up. For some people, that moment comes when they lose their job, their house, a much loved pet, or in really tragic circumstances, a member of their family. It's a sad, but increasingly 'usual response' to a life changing experience. The problem is, if you allow it to snowball and take hold, you can lose total control of dealing with even the smallest necessity. Gradually, you could find you've spent days, unwashed, without proper food, barely moving from your bed and you may even have extricated yourself entirely from any human interaction. This is how depression takes hold. If you can't tackle the fairly simple and fundamental aspects of your daily routine, then you won't be able to consider the more complex areas of life, which can stress us all out, even when we're in a good place. Being depressed, is a very real and all too often, tragic ramification of life in the twenty first century and nobody should ever feel guilty if they've had thoughts of simply pulling up the duvet over their heads, switching off the phones, locking the door, keeping the blinds closed and shutting out the outside world without any explanation to anyone.

There's been a handful of times I've felt that way in my life too, but however distraught I was, I instinctively knew that I had to take baby steps to fix one thing at a time. Something inside me never allowed that desperateness to go past a certain point. I always understood that if I could just get myself washed and dressed, it would be a sign that I wasn't crazy and I hadn't totally lost the plot. Don't strive for too much in one go, little improvements in restoring normality are major steps in getting yourself back in line with good health, both mentally and physically.

We should also never confuse feelings of hopelessness with that of being unable to cope, they're very dissimilar sentiments. Most of us feel unable to cope at some point in our crazy existences, but those who feel genuinely hopeless, often believe they have no way out of their predicament and that's why I express again in this book, that we always have choices. Even homeless, jobless, seemingly unloved drifters, have choices. Their options are way more limited than most of us, but there are still choices they have to make. They can either keep going, looking for any possible opening they can find in life, which will offer them the smallest opportunity back into the world, or they can give up, sleep on the streets in a haze of alcohol and any substances they can get their hands on and finish their lives as a statistic. I met numerous women at Crisis and the Prince's Trust charities, who were as down on their luck as you can get, but they refused to give up and after being offered a chance to enter an adult education programme, receive mentoring and begin the slow recovery of building up to a job and taking on some rented accommodation, however basic, they took it. Over time, some even started their own businesses and/or got jobs in London.

The bottom line is that we have to take some responsibility, even in a very depressed state, for not just how our life got to this point, but where it's going in the future. It's too simplistic to blame other people and circumstances for the situations we find ourselves in. Even if other people and fate have dealt us the worst possible hand, it's up to us to own our lives and make the right choices with or without destiny's influence.

Depression will also often hit us when our bodies are run down. Stress is a major factor in losing our ability to cope, but lack of nourishment or too much alcohol, can have an accumulative effect as well. It's all too easy to grab food on the hoof when we have such manic schedules, but I learned back in my early thirties, that eating well and cooking fresh food every night, rather than takeaway or microwave meals, was the only way

I could survive and be well enough to get through my exigent lifestyle. I've been a huge advocate of home cooked, natural food, for as long as I can remember and I discovered, through experience, that when my body was under attack, my mind would naturally deteriorate. Don't be under any illusion that the mind and body are isolated entities, as they're inseparably linked. If you think back to any times in your life when you've felt unwell with the flu, stomach bugs, sore throats, ear infections, abscesses, or general non-threatening illnesses we all go through, you'll know you couldn't have coped with normal stress or activities when your body was weakened. When you're fighting even the simplest of infections and your immune system is under attack, you can rarely face getting out of bed, never mind dealing with a hectic schedule. At a time when your body requires rest and recuperation, you simply can't manage pressure and or challenging situations.

Therefore, in order to handle the magnitude of life challenging events we go through, many on a regular basis, we have to keep our bodies in the best of health for our coping mechanism to sustain us in all areas. Depression is often the beginning of a run-down body losing its power to balance the very demanding routines we ask it to deal with on a daily basis. Stop eating junk, cleanse your body with a detox programme and then change your pattern of eating to include whole foods, fresh fruit and vegetables. Eliminate caffeine (which is also a stimulant and can increase anxiety enormously in those susceptible) and try, wherever possible, to use natural products in your home and on your face and body. Where you can, ensure you ALWAYS turn off Wi-fi when you sleep (from your router and on your mobile phone) as your body is repairing itself at night, so having harmful radiation waves blitzing you (and most especially your children) during that crucial rest time, is not to be recommended. We're already bombarded with numerous chemicals, pesticides, unwanted antibiotics in animals, hormones in water and a multitude of other dangerous and weakening influences that can affect us, so without being obsessive about what we eat, drink and how we live, there are things we can do to support our bodies in coping much better and reduce those traumas enormously.

Another change affecting us all and how we live, which has ultimately upset the natural balance of our world, is this instantaneous approach to everything we're involved in. I've seen (and felt) the very prolific transformation over the last thirty years, of our expectations demanding immediacy in all we do. That means that my daughter's generation has grown up in an environment of instant results, rapid conclusions and prompt responses in all aspects of their lives. Even though it's a different era to the one I was born in, I also find myself expecting this same immediacy in certain quarters, such as reaching a person over the weekend, who once upon a time, would have been out of contact after a Friday afternoon. When I first began work at Le Maitre, nobody reached colleagues or staff on Saturdays and certainly never on a Sunday, unless you had their home number and you'd only ever use that in a real emergency. Nowadays, if someone doesn't answer their mobile phone after a few rings on a Sunday, it's normal protocol to leave a voice mail, text them, call their home or other number provided, send an e-mail, WhatsApp or even tweet them!

There's no downtime anymore and no real 'switch off' mode for any of us. It's the times we live in and it's the acceptable way of doing business and most of us don't have a choice but to adhere to being available at all times, if we want to compete and offer the service our customers expect. The problem is, this culture of fixing everything in a heartbeat, carries over into the core of everything we now do and affects our thinking and responses. Never allowing ourselves time to be away from the pressures of every-day tensions, adds further weight to our already manic and stressful lives. It's just another reason why I don't believe that anti-depressants help the long term challenge of dealing with misfortunes, although, as indicated, I believe they do have their place in very specific instances.

My major concern about anyone taking these drugs, is that I genuinely feel being despondent is a symptom of life, which can't be eradicated by a magic dose of feel good chemicals. If you try and expel misery or hard times from your life, then you're living in a false existence which will lack balance. Good and bad, happy and sad, productive and unproductive, rich and poor, healthy and sick, all these opposites allow us to find a place somewhere in the middle of the seesaw. Nobody's happy all the time, healthy forever, successful without failures, rich without having had tough times (unless they're born very wealthy) and anyone who's been blessed with the good fortune of being born into a privileged family, sadly often finds tragedy has presented itself in one way or another, almost to demonstrate that this is simply life's way of ensuring there's a balance. I believe that as a society, we have to stop making it so easy for people to avoid going through, what are essentially, normal emotions and events.

If you watch any species in the animal world that teach their young to hunt, they allow their offspring to make mistakes. It's how they grow and learn. Some will die doing it, but generally there's an element of allowing the student to acquire the skills needed to fend for itself, while attempting to keep it out of danger. What the animal world most definitely doesn't do, is wrap it's young in cotton wool and protect them from harm's way. In the western world, we've become obsessed with solving all our children's issues (I'm no different and have been as much to blame as anyone) but I don't think we've done our kids, or the next generation, any favours by doing so. Putting young people on anti-depressants for instance, is condoning that a generation should seek medical intervention as soon as the going gets tough. Before people start sending hate mail because they disagree vehemently with my views and want to tell me about how these pills have helped them through difficult times, I'm not condemning or judging anyone who's taken, or is still taking this type of medication. Some may genuinely, desperately, need them, along with any other assistance they can receive from the medical profession. All I'm saying, is that before doctors reach for their prescription pads, shouldn't we consider looking, as a society, about why so many people require drugs to get them through life? Just like doctors gave out too many antibiotics years ago and ultimately we're now struggling with superbugs that are becoming resistant to them (not to mention the millions of people who are walking about suffering from Candida as a result) are we not setting ourselves up for a similar disaster with anti-depressants? I recently got bitten by an insect while abroad and contracted Cellulitis so I urgently needed antibiotics, as without them, I could've developed Septicemia and died. I was therefore extremely grateful this medication was available to me, so of course we're all fortunate to have access to drugs that can help save our lives when required, but I'm sure I was given antibiotics many times over the years when they weren't totally necessary and I'm lucky they still worked when I really needed them.

If people, especially the young, are given drugs so easily to get them through relatively tough times, what happens when real life changing events occur that totally rock their world? How equipped will they be to cope with the heartrending tragedies they may have to face if these medications are so easily accessible and this false ability to handle issues is part of their normal existence? When a person's receptor sites no longer react to the strength of drug they're on, they'll require stronger ones to keep them feeling they can cope with life in general, so it doesn't take a genius to work out what happens eventually. It isn't just medication that's losing us balance, it's partly this blame culture we live in, always expecting someone else to take the responsibility and therefore the consequences of our actions. Bad schools aren't responsible for our children misbehaving inside and outside the classroom, they're accountable for teaching and educating our kids, but parents have to take full and absolute responsibility, for their children's behaviour. Governments aren't liable when our kids go out, get drunk and then hi-jack a car, or act in an antisocial way and yet so many blame whichever party is in power for easy access to cheap alcohol, pornography, violence and a thousand other things, which may've influenced our offspring to take that destructive route. We have to start being accountable for our own actions and those still in our care and in turn, we need to pass on that same set of values to our children, who'll continue the lineage of mature childrearing.

Many of us have protected our children a little too much, as has today's society in general and as a result, we've elicited a culture where patience, commitment and long term planning, isn't always something this generation adopts easily. The instant route to fame, fortune and celebrity status, that so many stumble upon today, has in some way denigrated the decades of hard work our forefathers put in to pave the way for our success. The blood, sweat and tears our previous peers went through to achieve a better life for their families, is somehow diluted by the immediacy of this generation's triumphs. Furthermore, it promotes a culture of resentment for those who do have to work hard, against those who access such an easy path to their dreams. I love to see people achieve outstanding success and I aspire, as most people do, to mirror those who've reached their goals through sheer resilience, but it's difficult to respect anyone who doesn't work hard or show their obligation to finish what they started.

If we could slow down just a little bit and remove ourselves from the treadmill of life, maybe we'd learn to appreciate the health and happiness we're granted and be content in the moment. There's nothing wrong with striving for the affluence most of us desire, but constantly chasing the next deal, doesn't always allow us to understand that spiritual enlightenment, can be far more rewarding than monetary recompense alone. If we want to restore balance in our manic lives, then as a society in general, we need to be more grateful for what we do have and less angry about what we don't have. Going back to basics, living as one with nature, appreciating the simple pleasures, are just some of the ways to restore the stability which is so often missing for us all, in the first quarter of this century. If we could find a way to access the excitement and challenges we crave, while valuing the regular routines we often come to resent, we might actually be closer to acquiring the equipoise, which seems to elude us in our daily regimes.

While many of us yearn for excitement in our lives, we also, in contrast, like to stay in our comfort zones where everything is safe and familiar. Nobody likes the uneasiness of situations that challenge us where we feel vulnerable and unsure how we might respond and cope. Over the years, I've found it fascinating to watch reality programmes like Strictly Come Dancing or Dancing on Ice, where a celebrity takes on a new challenge and is under pressure, in the spotlight. When a contestant does well, it's clearly one of the most rewarding experiences of their lives and the adulation and praise is like a drug that spurs them on to do even better the following week. However, those who get it badly wrong and receive criticism, which is sometimes quite cutting and hurtful, are clearly deflated, visually, in front of the cameras.

What a different experience it is for those who rise to the challenge, conquer a new skill and excel in an unknown field, compared to the people who feel they've failed and embarrassed themselves on national TV (especially those who are already adored for a different discipline). This proves, that even individuals, who are already fairly successful in their particular subjects, still hunger after the recognition that great achievement brings, but in order to reach those giddy heights of admiration and approval, they have to go through an uncomfortable process of not knowing if they'll attain their goals or not. Some will simply never try, because they'll consider that taking on something new, which they don't know if they're going to succeed in, is far too risky. Other's will give something a go and find it an amazing and fulfilling experience, but those who take on the challenge and fail, can find it much harder to come to terms with than never trying at all.

This is when I believe you need to look inside yourself and not give up. It's all too easy to say you tried and it never worked so you're never going to expose yourself to that risk again. That's precisely the time you need to take another chance and that's exactly the moment when you have to dig deep and visualize the success and not the failure that your next venture might bring. The key to attainment is belief and faith and not giving up at the first sign of difficulty or even at the tenth sign of it! I believe that everybody fails at something they do in their lives, at some point. The law of averages, with its rule of outcomes and probabilities will bear that out and if you read any autobiography on the world's most successful people, you'll find it to be true. Yet, once you do succeed at something, it brings a much better chance of further success, which is why many of the greatest entrepreneurs the world has produced, often move into hugely diverse businesses after their first foray and yet still accomplish in other chosen industries. It's naturally far easier to increase wealth and success once we have it and that's due to many reasons. Firstly, money makes money, so after one successful enterprise, you generally obtain that hard to define 'credibility' component, which opens doors to all kinds of opportunities, including the chance to have people invest in your ideas. Then there's the option to borrow money more easily to finance a new deal, which is always one of the most difficult parts of any business, especially for those starting out on their first, commercial, endeavour. You also have the experience of a company, which has been successful, giving insight and a degree of expertise into the pitfalls of what can go wrong in any firm, large or small. Finally, in my opinion, you have the confidence in your own abilities from all you've learned in your previous venture and that's never to be underestimated. All these aspects, increase positivity, bringing a 'feel good' factor with it and people naturally want to be around those who are positive and believe in themselves and what they're doing.

Nobody wants to invest in a person who's likely to panic and give up as soon as complications arise. If someone is going to be your partner, whether it's a friend, a bank, or a venture capitalist, they'll want a return on their money. They'll also want to know that the person at the helm, whom they're trusting with their investment, is going to be much like the captain of an airplane – steady, reliable capable and someone who remains calm and controlled during turbulent times. Most importantly, a person who's going to stay on board and land the plane in extreme difficulties, not parachute out to save himself and let the plane go down.

All those qualities are important if you want to succeed and you may not think you possess them and never will, but I don't believe that's true. I'm convinced we all have much more strength of character in us then most of us know but if you don't put things to the test, you'll never find out what you are capable of, or what attributes you really do own.

In 2012, I took on something called the 'Costa Rica Challenge' for the Prince's Trust. It was to raise money for underprivileged kids and teenagers in the UK. I knew when I agreed to do it with a bunch of close friends that it would be tough, but I can honestly say, I had no idea, just how extreme and intense it would be. I wrote this e-mail the day after I got home to all those who had supported me:

Dear Family, Friends and Colleagues,

I've just returned from my trip to Costa Rica and never has my home been a more welcome sight! For all of you who so kindly sponsored me, I wanted to at least try and relay the experience as best I could. To say it's been life changing is an understatement! As you know, I had a severe knee injury which stopped me training for two months before my trip and after a painful Cortisone injection I left the UK not knowing if the knee would hold up or not.

After a twenty three hour journey, two hours sleep and a six hour time difference, we were bussed straight into the jungle to begin our trek. Although we're hardly strangers to rain, nothing could've prepared us for the force and relentlessness of the downpours in Costa Rica. Even with waterproofs it was impossible to stay dry. Furthermore, with the intense humidity, waterproofs just made us sweat more and overheat, so we all opted to get soaked from day one onwards. The terrain was the most unforgiving imaginable and was literally uphill for most of the eight hours per day over the six days we trekked. There were no moderate inclines, just vertical hills. No sooner did we get to the top of one hill when we rounded a corner and another came into view. The only respite from this upward route march was when we went deeper into the jungle and the terrain became 'one man' trails which had to be climbed rather than walked. These were much more treacherous and demanding and at times, as hard as the hills had been, I wished for their return! Our camps were all totally washed out from the extreme rain conditions and after returning, up to our thighs in mud, to whatever relatively dry camps were provided, we'd occasionally be offered a freezing cold, outdoor shower which we'd have to take surrounded by spiders and snakes. We'd then dress in damp clothes as it was impossible to keep anything dry the entire time we were there. Our boots were totally sodden as we had to wade through rivers and on one day had to form a human chain to get everyone across safely. For the first three days, I was sick from the Malaria tablets and was unable to eat. After burning some 3 – 4,000 calories per day and only managing to consume around 800, my weight started to visibly drop off me and I lost around six pounds in forty eight hours making it really tough to keep up my energy levels. This coupled with carrying a rucksack that weighed around four fifths of my body weight added to the challenge. The doctor on the trek gave me anti sickness pills and gradually I began to eat again.

The e-mail I sent everyone originally explaining I'd been told the spiders were the size of dinner plates was a slight misrepresentation. They were more like serving dishes and I attach a photo of one grey Tarantula which was in our camp along with a much larger black one that I couldn't even face photographing! On the two intense days we climbed the one man trails in torrential rain, we had to be very careful not to fall sideways as not only were we climbing extremely steep, unsteady and narrow passages, covered in leaves, tree roots and thick mud with big drops behind us, but there were hundreds of the most enormous ant hills which would cover you in seconds if you fell. There were also snakes spiders and every creepy crawly imaginable alongside us every step of the way. The hardest part was catching your breath as you couldn't stop for even a few seconds because the ants would cover your boots and get up between your gaiters and bite relentlessly. I literally look as though I've contracted chicken Pox as I was eaten alive by ants and mosquitos. However much repellent you put on, with the extreme sweat it was washed away within half an hour. You'll note some of the photos of me look like an advert for why you should use Tenor Lady as it appears I've lost control of my bladder but it's simply another day of extreme sweating in humidity which was almost 100%! I pushed myself to physical limits I could never *have envisaged getting through before I went. It was an unbelievably gruelling schedule even for the young members of the group but for the older contingent it was seriously tough. When I was told we couldn't white water raft as two people had died the day before we were due to attempt it, because the rivers were simply too swollen and dangerous, I was actually disappointed. I would have happily jumped into a raft (one of my greatest fears of the challenge!) to save my legs from another exhausting day of walking as the fatigue was indescribable. There were many times I wondered if we were in fact not really on a Prince's Trust Challenge but an undercover training mission for the Green Berets as I can't imagine, apart from the combat, that their training could be much harder!*

Finally, on the last day of blood sweat and tears we rounded a hill to see the finishing post in sight. There had been lots of tears from various people during the difficult challenge but I hadn't been one of them. However, as I crossed the finishing line representing the end of the toughest physical week of my life, the tears flowed freely! Other than the day my daughter was born I can honestly say it was the most elation I've ever felt.

That night we had a Gala dinner and I am so proud to say that with the 20 people I trekked with, I won the award for 'spirit of the week' for being the toughest trooper and the tiny wooden box with the inscription, along with the medals we all won for completing the challenge, will now be amongst my most prized possessions.

I want to thank everyone, from the bottom of my heart for not only the amazing financial commitment many of you made but for the moral and emotional support you've given me to complete the task. You have genuinely helped to change the lives of so many underprivileged and homeless kids and in the process, changed mine forever.

Thank you so, so much to all those who've donated and if anyone who hasn't but would still like to make a small donation for all those kids who kept me going while I was out there, my just giving page is still live and I enclose the link below.

God Bless and thank you all.

Karen xxx

I didn't realize the response I would get from sending that e-mail, but apparently many people cried when they read it and as a result, my pledges increased. My only intention when forwarding it, was to simply express, in the best way I could, my emotions the day I got home, and to share, with all those people who'd supported me, my journey, while it was still fresh in my mind. The trip had been such a huge thing for me to have accomplished and was truly an experience of a lifetime, which I never want to repeat, but which I'll always be eternally grateful for completing.

The best part was knowing that I'd genuinely put myself in a situation that was way out of my comfort zone in every way imaginable and I had gotten through it. The doctor on the trek had tried to convince me the week before, not to attempt it, as I hadn't trained enough due to my injury and of course there was no way of knowing if the injection in my knee had worked and if it hadn't, I would've been in real trouble climbing that terrain. My friends all suggested the same and said they'd totally understand if I pulled out with such an injury, so I had the perfect opportunity not to go and I would still have raised the money, as nobody was going to take back the pledges they'd made at that stage.

There was a large part of me that would've loved not to go and camp outside in the rain forest with the biggest and most deadly spiders and snakes on the planet, or put my body through the most gruelling of challenges at my age, but I knew I'd regret it if I didn't go, as I would have been taking the line of least resistance and giving up simply because I had an excuse to fail. Taking part, taught me so many things about myself and about life in general.

I remember my dear friend, Val, who'd been on two previous challenges with the Prince's Trust, laughed at me when I told her I was taking a solar phone charger so I could answer my e-mails every evening after the day's trekking. I had no idea what she found so funny at the time, until I was in the jungle and realized how ludicrous my thoughts had been. Not only was there virtually no signal at most of the stops we made, but I barely thought of what was going on in the UK during the entire week, let alone considered sending or checking e-mails. I'm almost ashamed to say, that from day one until the night of the gala dinner, I barely thought about my daughter, partner, family or my business, other than a brief, fleeting consideration, the only thought in my mind was survival. It had been made clear during the briefing we'd been given at the start of the trek, that we had to take responsibility for ourselves and our own safety. We were going to be deep in the jungle, with all manner of dangers and we weren't going to be babysat. Our guides told us that the trek before ours, had consisted of around twenty doctors and apparently one of the women on the trip had been stung by a hornet. She had a severe allergic reaction and went into anaphylactic shock so they used an EpiPen on her, but she never responded. It took six EpiPens to save her and the only reason they had that number available, was because it was a doctor's convention. Had there been just the one doctor, as we had trekking with us, carrying limited supplies, she would have died. That was enough for me to focus my mind on the task at hand and stop worrying about what was going on in the much safer environment of the UK!

It was a real revelation to me how naturally I, and my dearest friends, Sarah, Belinda, Val, Vanessa Lucia and all the other people I trekked with, switched into survival mode and concentrated entirely on what was required. Even more revealing, was how twenty alpha females got on so incredibly well without a single disagreement the entire trip, showing only solidarity and great support for each other. I was so proud to have met such an amazing bunch of women, the majority of whom, led very privileged lives, but were willing to put their bodies through a gruelling program in some very uncomfortable situations, to help young homeless people get out of poverty. It proved to me that if ordinary working women (many of them middle aged) who had no experience of camping on a holiday site (never mind doing so in a jungle!) were able to adapt, not just their minds, but their physical capabilities, to achieve something so demanding, there's nothing to stop anyone from reaching their goal in life, whatever age they are. As long as you're living and breathing, you're capable of doing extraordinary things.

CHAPTER 6

THINKING OUTSIDE THE BOX

While my partners and I were going through the court case in Canada, typically, an amazing opportunity came up for our company to purchase another business, also in Canada, which was one of our largest clients. It was an incredible entity that had huge prospects and a real synergy with Le Maitre. As with everything else in life, timing can alter a lot of major decisions and we all agreed that being in the middle of litigation was not the optimum time to expand our operations. I recognized it as an exceptional opportunity and with the approval of the other directors, I went about finding backers who would invest in me buying the business personally, with an agreement that while running the new company in Canada, I could still be part of Le Maitre. Looking back, it was a very ambitious project to undertake, but I was passionate about this particular company and I knew, if it came off, it would be a brilliant career move and give me an incredibly fulfilling role in a new environment. Furthermore, it would've allowed me to realize some of my aspirations, by running a company in its entirety, instead of having to make decisions by committee, which is the normal protocol when you're in business with several partners.

I was truly grateful that my fellow directors gave me their blessing to embark on the opportunity and in hindsight, it was more than gracious of them, as although I wasn't abandoning ship, I was certainly putting all my efforts and focus on a different company which was of no benefit, at that time, to them or the company, at all.

After finding a backer and going through all the due diligence, financials and contract agreements, which took months of work, we were finally decided on all matters relating to the purchase and I'd negotiated myself a great deal. Unfortunately, on the day of signing, when I was due to fly to Canada to take over the company, the exchange fell through at the eleventh hour, through absolutely no fault of my own and I was left with a six figure debt and had lost the company I desperately wanted to buy. I was angry, upset and totally mystified at how it could've gone so horribly wrong, but thankfully, the owners gave me a second chance to find new backers, even though they had a company waiting in the wings to purchase them.

I immediately started investigating opportunities to put another deal together and within a week or so, I'd found a group of people to assist me. After lots of initial meetings, we were once again on track to go through with the purchase a second time. This transaction was considerably more complex and had a far larger number of people involved as a result. It was also a much more intelligent deal and due to the way it had been structured, far less debt would be incurred, as it was connected to money being raised in the city, on a company which was already on the AIM market.

In theory, it should have worked out perfectly, but a member of the team brought in a reasonably well known individual in the entertainment industry to assist with raising the profile of the company, in order to stimulate more interest from the city investors. The man, who was introduced to the project late in the proceedings, decided to hijack the deal and then managed to sabotage it, through his ineptitude and greed. I remember the lawyer who had handled all the employment contracts and other necessary legal agreements for the purchase in Canada, on both the first and second deal, was so kind to me and very sympathetic when he explained, that in all his years of practicing law, he'd never seen more bad luck than I'd experienced in both deals failing, over matters which were completely outside my control.

There are several aspects to this story which are really important for me to relay, as they fit in with so many points I've raised during the earlier part of this book. At the time of losing the company twice, which then got purchased by an investment company that had been quietly waiting to acquire it from the beginning, I lost almost half a million dollars and for a short time, my reason for getting out of bed in the morning. I'd put so much energy into trying to buy that particular business, that it had been almost my entire focus for well over eighteen months. After the collapse of both deals, I had no clue how to move forward with my life, having had a massive loss to both my pocket and my self- esteem. Even harder, was trading on a daily basis with the company I'd been unsuccessful in buying, as it's still to this day, a large customer of Le Maitre. It was a constant and painful reminder, that all my efforts to acquire it had failed miserably and in the process, I'd squandered a vast sum of money too.

If ever there was a time I felt like giving up, it was in the weeks following my aborted attempt to twice acquire the Canadian enterprise. The very thought of having to go through further litigation so soon after our two year court battle in Canada, made me feel physically ill, but doing nothing simply wasn't an option. I therefore set about embarking on yet another mission, by preparing the evidence to take action against the parties involved in the two separate deals, which had both been unsuccessful due to the failure of others. This was not a straightforward or cut and dried situation, but I spent weeks collating paperwork, gathering e-mails, notes and text messages and generally assembling the necessary proof required to bring a lawsuit against the people who were culpable for me losing, not just the money, but an amazing opportunity as well.

I cannot disclose, for legal reasons, what the terms of the settlement were, but I can confirm that even after being told, yet again, it was unlikely I had a strong case for obtaining any money from those responsible, I took on two difficult and complex legal challenges and won them both separately, this time, without going to court.

The litigation in Canada, taught me that if you have integrity and are prepared to go through thousands of documents to prove you played with a straight bat and other people, through greed or incompetence, were willing to risk your money in a cavalier fashion, ignoring their commitments and showing no duty of care, then you have no choice but to seek justice from those accountable. I hired a great lawyer, who interestingly enough, asked me on both occasions, to put my own case forward to those I was suing, along with their legal counsel. He was quite insistent that if I could articulate my position to those I was fighting, anywhere near as adamantly as I'd done to him, he believed they'd settle.

Which proves one thing alone, if you're passionate about being right and you're genuine about seeing something though to the end, like litigation, then the game of bluff is removed from the equation and that's often what the intrinsic core of suing someone comes down to. At the beginning of the case, I received more than one letter from the other side's legal representatives, threatening, that if I continued to take action, I'd be counter sued and financially ruined, which is the game solicitors play in order to make the weak back down. Although that tact may often work, in my case, it simply lit a fuse and made me twice as determined to see things through to the end and have my day in court. Once the opposition knows you mean business, they'll rarely take the fight inside a courtroom. Remember, when people know they're in the wrong, they will naturally try and be as aggressive as they can. Attack is the oldest and best form of defence and frightens many people into submission, but being right, being honest and fair, is what will get you through these situations.

The only reason the lawyer asked me to put my own case forward, was to ensure that it didn't just come down to legal counsel relying on the best prosecution/defence tactics. He explained, that if I rationalized my belief in the case as fervently as I had when I went to see him, the other side would see there was little point in all the time consuming posturing that goes on before an agreement's reached. He felt they'd see immediately, that I was set on going to court and unless they offered a fair and reasonable settlement, there'd be no other option than to have the case heard by a judge. So although he was far more intellectual and knowledgeable about these matters than I was, he knew that speaking on my behalf wouldn't demonstrate the determination and belief I had to see it through to the end.

This goes back to previous chapters about never giving up on your dreams and never allowing yourself to be a victim. You have choices. They can be tough, just like mine were, but they're still choices which we're all able to make in this free egalitarian world we live in. I could've lost a lot more money in fees than I might have won, but in my heart, I had the courage of my convictions and knew I could win. Losing wasn't an option and therefore I never entertained the thought. I constantly visualized victory until I could literally taste it. Negativity has no place in litigation. Belief, courage and determination have everything to do with winning, not just in court, but in life as well.

Several years on from those events, it became clear to me that there was a reason I never obtained the company I wanted. I believe I was destined to have the opportunity to run Le Maitre without restrictions and since taking on that challenge, we've been growing at between twenty five and thirty five percent per year. That doesn't mean I know more than my partners did, or are better at business, I'm not. It simply means I have the drive to push forward harder and faster than they did. Having partners can be a wonderful asset and it's always good to have people to bounce ideas off and share responsibilities with, but it can also be restrictive and time consuming when you have to arrange meetings to agree on changing, or improving, even the smallest process.

My brother-in-law is now the perfect partner and gives me all the support I need, without any of the obstructions a 'committee run' business brought with it. He respects my decisions and is excited by the new energy the company has taken on since changing the dynamics in the last couple of years. He started, with my father, an incredible and amazing business and brought in some outstandingly talented people some of whom are still with us today, which in turn gave me a life changing opportunity. I've never been happier and understand that I was not meant to succeed in buying another entity or leaving Le Maitre. If I'd put all my energies into the company I tried to buy and not our family business, my brother-in-law would've been left, all these years later, with the full burden of running the company, without really wanting that role at this time in his life and that doesn't make for a successful, or happy business.

I finally feel like the destructive situations, which arose through being in litigation, one way or another, for years on end, have taught me so much and have made me stronger, fairer and more capable of dealing with unplanned eventualities. I've also been made aware that 'thinking outside the box' about all situations, is rarely our first, or initial response to any problem as we all tend to centre on a much smaller framework, but having opened my mind to consider resolutions with far reaching outcomes, my outlook has been broadened and with it, my ability to find solutions that aren't always the obvious ones. It's not dissimilar to doing crossword puzzles, the more often you complete them, the quicker you'll derive those answers each time and the less complex they become. When looking to solve any issue, it's much easier to reflect on the simplest ways to deal with the problem, but that will rarely give you an advantage in business. Contemplating a different rationale to everyone else, is what will make you and your company, or brand, unique. If it was easy, everyone would be doing it. Trying to stretch yourself, by deliberating ways to succeed that are outside your normal sphere of consciousness, is how you grow and learn. Thinking outside the box, can help in so many aspects of life and allows you to view business, people and relationships with an alternative perspective to others.

Over the years, apart from my own marriage and relationships, I've been very close to various couples who have struggled to find a compromise to what they see as 'fundamental differences' between them that aren't easily solved. For example, I know one couple, where the wife was bordering on OCD about keeping the house and garden tidy and the husband was incredibly laid back, so domestic chores simply weren't a priority for him when the weekends came around. Although this kind of situation hardly seems insurmountable, or appears likely to threaten a strong marriage, it's amazing just how much of an issue it causes eventually, when a wife wants the lawn cutting and her husband wants to watch Formula One racing on a Sunday instead. I remember being with them on one occasion when this very argument erupted, which had clearly been a regular biting point for several years.

It appeared they both felt it quite advantageous that I was in residence and so took the opportunity to put their side of the argument to me in the hope I'd pick a team, giving a clear winner to the debate. Having found myself in the unenviable position of playing devil's advocate, I listened to each one dispassionately and came up with, what I believed, was a reasonable solution to satisfy both parties.

It seemed that not only was there real concern with the fact that this couple wanted such different things at the weekend, but the problem was exacerbated because they never saw each other much in the week and then spent the weekends arguing about not wanting to do the same things when they were together! I asked them why they didn't consider a simple compromise and spend Saturday doing all the things the wife wanted in the house, together, so that they tackled the cleaning and gardening most of the day. Then in the evening, they could relax with a nice meal and a bottle of wine and on Sunday spend the day chilling together, walking, watching TV or enjoying being in the garden.

It was strange, because the wife would happily have worked the entire weekend and didn't really want the 'chill' time at all. She found it difficult to slow down and relax and wanted to be on the go constantly and the husband was the exact opposite and having worked hard all week, wanted to do very little at the weekend but relax. The compromise I suggested just wouldn't have entered their thought processes, because neither were looking to make concessions. The wife wanted the husband to work every weekend, both Saturday and Sunday and the husband wanted to relax both days at the weekend, after working hard and travelling long distances in his job. Eventually, they did adopt the idea of this arrangement and realized that it could actually work, especially if they did the chores together, as it cut the time in half and meant they had a full day in each other's company, albeit, working in the house and garden.

They found that an advantage of operating as a close team on one of their days off, meant it afforded them a second full day where they could totally do whatever they wanted, without the pressure of the tasks building up. The husband actually came to like the 'togetherness' they shared when working for a common goal and the wife stopped 'nagging' and came to look forward to those lazy Sunday's, where she no longer felt guilty about having time off from her duties. Not a complex solution in any way, but they'd spent years arguing over the same issue and not once did they consider finding a settlement that would work for them. They were both highly intelligent people but because they didn't allow themselves to think outside the box, and more importantly, didn't want to show weakness in their arguments and concede anything, they failed to determine any meaningful resolve. This is why it's so important to weigh up all options, be fair minded and be prepared to give, in order to receive. If you think only about what you want to achieve, without incentivizing others to help you get there, you will never reach your goals, however big or small. Negotiation and compromise, are both major keys to success, in all areas of our lives. We spend way too much time thinking those phrases only apply to work and business and yet if we could open our minds and see that even in our closest relationships, perhaps we should learn to find compromises, more so at times than we do with our business colleagues, then maybe our personal lives would be so much smoother. I also try to remind myself regularly, that while fate may afford us certain opportunities, it's our own sense of purpose and will to succeed, both personally and professionally, that dictates how we utilise the significant chances we're ultimately provided with.

CHAPTER 7

BRINGING HOME THE BREAD

One of the greatest challenges facing couples today, is learning to deal with the fact the numerous women in relationships have become the breadwinners and many men either don't work and have taken on the role of house husband, or earn less than their partner. While this shouldn't really be relevant in the twenty first century, it's still one of the most testing issues couples deal with in the second decade of this new Millennium.

The reason it shouldn't be relevant, is that as long as both partners are making a contribution to the relationship and the home, it doesn't matter how it's achieved. However, many men are still of the opinion that they need to provide for their families and that's a natural instinct and an attractive quality in a man. Most females aren't adverse to that response, but when the man in their life believes he must be the main bread winner or he's failing, then there's a problem. I wish men could understand that it honestly doesn't make any difference to a woman who earns the most. If she's committed to you then she loves you and doesn't care. What she does care about, is that you still make her feel protected, treasured and most of all, attractive. If you earn less, that is not a demonstration of your manhood, or prowess. It doesn't define you and most importantly, it shouldn't emasculate you but in so many cases it does, more because of men's insecurities than any reality being attached to its importance from a woman's point of view.

Even if a woman does her best to ensure her man still feels capable and confident, she can't do it on her own and needs the man to believe it genuinely doesn't matter to the marital home if he's the major earner or not. Again, there's only so much that can be achieved in theory, but in practice, this is a really complicated problem and I've found it to be one of the biggest threats to a happy, contented, relationship.

Many people over the years have asked me, what, in my opinion, is the most important element, in any marriage or partnership holding firm and getting through the challenging times. I've never wavered in my staunch belief that there's just one essential ingredient that will save every relationship from fading and will allow both sides to keep the same level of attraction they had from day one. It may sound a little sanctimonious to make such a strong statement, but I truly believe that women certainly, if they dared to consider a genuine response to what they want most from any relationship, it's this one principal factor that can sustain or deplete their world in a heartbeat. 'Respect' for the person they love, is the magnet that will bond couples, long after the initial, physical, attraction has gone. Receiving respect from their partner has the same effect. Nevertheless, respect should never be 'a given' nor should it be taken for granted, once it's been achieved. It has to be earned and so very often, you can lose respect for a partner because of how they act or respond to situations. In the same way that respect is something which is achieved over time, it can be lost over time also, but men should be aware that once a woman starts to lose it for her partner, it rarely revives itself and is often the point at which she seeks solace elsewhere or simply shuts down from wanting to be in the partnership. I've known so many couples, where due to the men earning less than the women, the men have, in their own ways, started to try and take control over the smallest of issues. In order to feel more important and in essence, behave like 'the man of the house', yielding important decisions, they've shown unreasonable responses and used excessively forceful arguments, to win a small victory. The problem with this, is its neither masculine nor will it command respect from your partner.

As equals, you should always make decisions together and

trying to put your foot down about the little things simply to make a point and attempting to be more assertive because you're not the breadwinner, ends up being a childish and less manly thing to do, than showing love and support to your partner. This is a prime example of men not understanding what women need and is one of the biggest mistakes they can ever make in a relationship. Women want support at home. They want to feel loved, cherished, attractive and valued. Their opinion matters and they want to share it with the man they love. They want to talk about important topics and make decisions together. They want to divulge their insecurities without feeling they're trivial. They want to show their strength and not feel unfeminine in doing so. They want a man who looks up to them, respects them, but most importantly, allows them to be who they are without ever feeling they shouldn't have let their guard slip. Who earns the money is rarely important to a woman, but having a man she can depend and rely upon and who makes her feel like a sex goddess in bed and the most engaging woman on earth, at the dinner table, is as good as it gets.

Never make the mistake that she wants you to take charge to show your masculinity, not when it's ignoring her wants and needs. Don't confuse that with thinking you should never make a reservation at her favourite restaurant, or surprise her with a special dinner at home, without her consent, as that's a good move! Making decisions that affect her life, especially ones that you're making purely to demonstrate your alpha male status and stamp your authority on the relationship, will end up having the opposite effect and will eventually make her question that very strength, which she'll see as a weakness rather than a quality to revere.

As I've said before, men are simple creatures and

unfortunately, women are incredibly complex in many ways, but the most interesting and thought provoking part of any journey between two people is to try and see the other's point of view. Most men want a woman who understands them, loves them, doesn't challenge their every decision, is sexually interesting to them and can demonstrate her ability to be a great wife and mother to his children. Lots of men, while loving the diversity a woman can show, struggle to handle all the facets of a female's personality and her strong needs and wants but remember, however complex a woman is, she longs for the basic qualities from a man which are loyalty, strength, dependability, honesty, integrity and a sense of humour. Of course lots of women would love a successful, rich, generous, good looking man with a physique like David Beckham, but the majority of women would never swap their man for anyone and will see him as her own Greek God, whatever his stature, if he's there for her, makes her happy, respects and loves her and stands by her through thick and thin.

Women today are earning far more than ever before, so this matter no longer affects the minority. If men don't learn how to deal with the love of their life being the breadwinner, or at least being on level terms with them financially, it will ultimately destroy many special and unique relationships. All because their male ego gets in the way and stops them being able to accept that they're an equally important part of the relationship, whether they bring home all the money or none at all.

In the forty nine years that my parents were married, my mother worked for just two of those, when she and a friend managed a shop my father opened. Nonetheless, she made a massive contribution to the marriage and although looking back, I see that at times she felt she had no real control because she didn't earn her own money, she in fact had way more than she could have ever imagined. My father would've been lost without her and when she died, his very obvious deterioration proved that to be true. She literally ran our home, brought up myself and my sister, cooked the food, made sure we had clean, ironed clothes, entertained their mutual friends and his business clients and was a constant support to my father in every way. She was the glue that held the family together and was the strength and backbone of our lives. That can't be measured in monetary value.

For women who are alone and have to achieve in business, run a home and bring up children without anyone to assist, it's hard to imagine a more imperative function for a man to play, than being her support structure. To be her one constant in a world of chaos, her rock when she's floundering, her permanent soul mate, giving stability to all she does, and yet men don't see that as an important role. Why would any man feel undermined to take on an incredibly difficult task, that's both demanding and fulfilling? Thankless at times, maybe, but then the most rewarding imaginable, when she comes home and tells you she couldn't face her life without your love and strength, that you've changed her existence forever and made her feel complete and capable of taking on the world with you by her side. Why would any man feel emasculated and inconsequential when he's giving his woman the most vital and critical tools with which to manage her life? By offering the fundamental, but necessary, basic requirements, such as love, affirmation and encouragement to your woman, you're giving her the very sustenance she needs to live and grow and she will love and respect you forever for that validation.

One of the things women desperately want when they're going through a hard time, is for a man to empathise with them.

This should never be confused with sympathy, as a woman doesn't want to be pitied, she wants to be understood. That's when a soul mate, partner, boyfriend, husband or whatever your other half is to you, comes into his own and proves beyond any shadow of a doubt, that he identifies with, and has compassion for, whatever his woman is going through. These are the true emotions that bond couples. Taking the time to learn and truly appreciate what the other is facing and how those particular troubles can affect you both, will bring you together as a collective unit. Dismissing your woman's emotions, simply because you can't identify with them, will ensure you drift further apart if not immediately, then over time. Women will always want girlfriends to talk to and depend upon for a shoulder to cry on, but deep down they crave that special bond with the man they love and the couples that can share those feelings, however hard they are to explain and discuss, will ultimately have a relationship, where they're not just lovers, but are best friends as well.

When respect starts to be lost for your partner, it's like watching a fading sunset – you can't stop it disappearing behind the hills, you can only stand and stare as it slowly vanishes from view. Don't let that happen. Go back to the basics of this book and find a way to talk and fix things. Listen to each other. Argue, fight, debate, but never avoid. Avoidance is the slow degenerative disease which kills the relationship, destroys all hope of understanding each other and will prevent you from growing old as a couple. We all change through the decades, sometimes at a different pace to our partner and our wants and needs shift too, but if we never talk about our dreams and aspirations, as they alter and evolve, we can't expect our partner to recognize those adjustments when they do occur.

Share your life, don't just dip in an out of each other's when it suits you. Learn to embrace your partner's failings along with his/her good qualities. Never be indifferent about anything, better to have strong feelings than none at all. Don't just tolerate each other; life together shouldn't be an endurance course, but a valued, mutual journey. Respect your partner's wants and needs, discuss your views and visions, keep the pillow talk going and above all, when you've had the fiercest argument you can imagine and you're filled with nothing but anger and derision for your loved one, never go to sleep at night without some gesture of forgiveness, even if it's brushing past their hand and touching it momentarily before you retire to separate rooms in a rage. Passion, whether it's strong love, or a moment of pure wrath, is our most affecting emotion. We can never take back what we say in the heat of the moment, we can only spend years repenting or making amends in some way, to absolve ourselves of the significance of our fulminations. Love and hate may be at opposite ends of the spectrum, but they make us crazy in equivalent degrees. Just remember that the person who makes you sing in the morning can just as easily make you scream by nightfall, but as long as your depth of feelings can be ignited by that person, whichever end of the spectrum it falls within, then they're worth fighting for and so is the relationship.

Finally, if and when you think you're close to falling into the trap of looking outside your relationship for comfort, try watching Fatal Attraction together. This should stand as a firm reminder that going off the rails can be as grave as in the Hollywood movies, only in the real world, there's unlikely to be a happy ending and it may not just be the bunny that winds up being boiled in the pot!

Printed in Great Britain
by Amazon.co.uk, Ltd.,
Marston Gate.